Neither Death nor Life:
Surviving and Thriving in the Unrelenting Crisis

by Nancy Jordan Unks

To Ralph, whose unconditional love prepared my heart for Christ's

Chapter 1 Shattered Lives Shatter Faith

"I don't understand why he keeps on living." My voice trembled, my eyes filled. In the weeks since Ralph's cerebral hemorrhage, I had done plenty of crying, but only with family or close friends. I did not want to break down in front of this stranger. "I saw the CAT scan," I continued. "That blood clot should have killed him. And all the complications since then..."

The psychologist handed me the box of tissues from her desk. I dabbed my eyes. She spoke softly, "It's easy to die. One simply stops living." There was a knock at the door, and someone beckoned her into the hall. Her words echoed in my ears as memories of recent events came to mind.

Ralph and I exchanging a parting kiss as we stood in the kitchen on a sunny, spring Saturday morning. "Are you sure you can be back in time?" I asked. "Yes, I promise," he answered. Then simultaneously, "Love you," as he went out the back door and I turned to the breakfast clean up.

CAT scan images dropping, one by one, into a bin in a dim hallway off the emergency entrance to Temple University Hospital. I recognized the cross section of the skull and brain. A bright, white area filled most of one hemisphere—a massive blood clot.

Alone in the office, I let the tears flow.

The neurosurgery resident standing outside the Intensive Care Unit a few days after Ralph underwent surgery to remove the clot: "We almost lost him during the night," he said. "His blood pressure dropped, and his temperature went up. He has pneumonia."

Ralph's hands resting on the white sheet of his hospital bed as he lay in a coma. Long fingers with traces of wood stain under the nails and calluses on the fingertips. Hands that built furniture, played the guitar, and tickled our two little daughters. Hands whose caress could both excite and comfort me. Standing at Ralph's bedside, I held those familiar hands. Their warmth exuded hope.

"It's easy to die. One simply stops living." I reached for another tissue, squeezed the teardrops from my eyes, and blew my nose. The counselor returned, expecting to console a grieving wife, and was surprised to see me not crying. "I step out for a minute and already you've regained your composure," she said.

"Ralph's not giving up, so I can't either." I would go on making the daily trip into the city to be with my husband. I would go on taking care of Jenny and Amy who terribly missed their Daddy. I would go on as long as Ralph did. "My grandfather said you can get used to anything if you do it long enough—even hanging."

The psychologist did not seem to appreciate the wry humor. She gave me a look of pity and concern. "You never get used to something like this."

That was in 1978. The only prayer I remember breathing during the agonizing hours of Ralph's brain surgery was that he would live so we could see our little girls grow up. We have, indeed, watched together as our daughters grew into lovely and caring young women. They graduated from college and left the nest. But, Ralph remained totally paralyzed and unable to speak. I became his fulltime care manager.

Some people tried to tell me what life would be like for us. I did not believe them. I was sure Ralph would recover. Maybe he would have minor residual effects from the brain hemorrhage. Maybe he would not be an electrical engineer any more, but that was okay. He liked to work with his hands. He could pursue his woodworking as a profession. He would still be my husband, my lover, my best friend. I could not imagine him living for more than 35 years as a locked-in quadriplegic. That would be a living death, an eternal hell, a condition that is neither death nor life.

As I write this book, I hope our story will help you in whatever challenges you face. My grandfather's encouraged me. He spoke from experience when he said you could get used to anything. The last thirteen years of his life, he commuted to work by trolley on a prosthetic leg. I remember sitting on his knee (the real one, because the other one could pinch) while he told tall tales. I remember him rolling up his sleeve and entertaining me with funny faces while Grandma gave him his insulin injection. I never heard either of them complain about the situation.

You will need more than inspiring stories, however. When our lives were shattered, so was our faith. God seemed distant and cruel. Why would he do this to us? Or to anyone? Spiritual questions sapped much of my emotional energy. People who offered scriptural Band-Aids and theological explanations did not console me. The books they gifted me with were mockery. The people who really helped cried with me. They gave practical assistance and joined me in an honest search for answers.

Those who best reinforced my shattered faith were also going through crises. In their lives, I saw the strength and peace I needed. I began to ask about and hunger for what they had. What they had was Jesus. Their stories helped me find hope, not in a healing, a church, a creed, or ritual, but in a person—Jesus Christ. Through Jesus, I have peace that does not come by my own effort. His Holy Spirit is power for dealing with daily life.

In 2008 as I began compiling this book, Ralph remained quadriplegic. He communicated by answering yes/no questions with a weak hand squeeze. When someone set up his Eyegaze Communication System, he could spell out brief thoughts or play a game using the movement of his eye. He would chuckle at a joke. Something really funny made him smile. He liked to watch TV. Having a visual focus helped his body stay more relaxed. When he was tense, muscle spasms and leg cramps became excruciating. Surgery on his feet a few years before and periodic nerve blocking treatments helped reduce the cramping. Except for occasional minor colds and infections, he was healthy.

I was feeling older. When I did Ralph's care, my hands and back ached. I didn't function very well on five or six hours of sleep any more. My glasses were for both reading and distance. I made endless lists to remember everything. I began taking an expensive prescription medication to suppress heart palpitations, but was thankful for help from Medicare. I began to consider long-term care options for us both.

Though declining physically, I continued growing in spirit: growing closer to Jesus who is my strength and my peace; growing in my reliance on him and trust in him. Ralph indicated that he was growing, also. He looked forward to Sunday morning worship and to prayer and Bible study with our home group from church. Over the years, I read Scripture and inspirational literature to him, and his responses encouraged my faith.

Ralph and I enjoyed our two grandchildren, Jenny's daughters. Ashley, the older, was very observant of Gramps and his care. On a visit when she was only two, she "helped" with Gramps' exercise. Volunteers came to do that almost every weekday. We used a lift to get Ralph down to a mat on the floor. Then we moved and stretched his limbs, rocked him and twisted him, and turned him on his stomach. It's called range-of-motion. Afterwards, we used the lift to put him back in his wheelchair.

On returning home, Ashley began a similar routine with her favorite bear. Jenny called to tell the story. "Mom, you should see what Ashley's been doing," Jenny said, excitement in her voice. "She spreads her blanket on the floor, lays bear in the middle of it, and moves his arms and legs all around. At first I couldn't figure it out, so I asked her, 'Ashley, what are you doing?' She said, 'Bear needs exercise.' And here's the best part. When she's done, she calls me to help her. We each grab two corners of the blanket and lift bear in it. Then, she insists we swing him back and forth a couple of times before we plop him into the doll stroller. She tucks the blanket around him and pushes him over to watch whatever she's playing with next. It's so cute!"

I pray that Ashley and her sister Kate will never have to deal with such disability. If they ever do, I hope their memories of

Gramps and Grammy will be a positive influence as my grandparents were for me. More important, I hope they will find a friend, helper, comforter, and sustainer in Jesus. And I hope they will have known Jesus long before a crisis arises, so they will be better able to face it than I was when Ralph was first stricken. That is why I am writing our story. May it help lead you to Jesus.

Chapter 2 Prelude to Tragedy--1978

Jenny and Amy were asleep. It was also way past bedtime for mommies and daddies. The aroma of cake baking in the oven was beginning to fill the kitchen. I puttered, while Ralph hung around watching and helping. We spread the tablecloth on the dining room table—the pink one for a little girl's birthday. Then we draped pink and yellow crepe paper streamers from the chandelier.

"Should I blow up balloons?" Ralph asked.

"No," I said, pulling party supplies from a drawer. "Amy really wants to be in on that. Better wait 'til tomorrow." I turned to him with a frown; "You *can* be back in time to do the balloons before the party?"

"Yes, I think so. Look, are you sure you don't mind if I do this thing tomorrow?"

I had been silently wishing he would not do "this thing" tomorrow. Not on Amy's birthday. When he asked, I melted. He really did care what I wanted, and I knew how excited he was about his project. "Well, I'll be taking the girls to their ballet class in the morning, so you might as well go. It's just that these projects always take longer than they do. Amy only wants Daddy to do her balloons. What if you don't get back before the party?"

"I'll be back. I promise. Dave says the tree is all ready to go. We'll take it straight to the sawmill, and I'll come right home. We don't have to wait for the lumber. We pick that up next week. I should be back between 10:30 and 11:00."

I sighed, "Okay," and began arranging paper plates, napkins and favors on the buffet.
Ralph watched for a minute or two, leaning against the doorframe, hands in pockets. "Guess there really isn't any more for me to do here. I'll go on upstairs," he said.

"I'll be up as soon as the cake's out of the oven." I heard him go up to the study and close the door. I knew he would probably turn on TV for something to do until I came up.

As I re-arranged party favors, I thought, with a twinge of guilt, *I really should be more enthusiastic about Ralph's sawmill expedition.* Other husbands' hobbies netted their wives smelly fish and lonely hours home alone. Ralph's woodworking produced beautiful and functional pieces of furniture. We had him at home with us, even if the machinery in the basement was noisy at times.

A co-worker had offered to give him half the lumber from his walnut tree, if Ralph would help take it to a sawmill. Ralph had been quietly ecstatic when he told me about it. "Walnut has a beautiful grain," he said. "I'll be able to make some really nice stuff with all that wood. Maybe we can finally build that sewing cabinet you've been wanting."

We. That was neat the way he said, "We can build." He always consulted me on his furniture designs, and, though he did all the work, he considered them joint projects. Now that the weather was warm enough, Ralph was anxious to get the walnut tree moved so he would have the lumber to work with over the summer. *Why can't I share his excitement?*

The dinging oven timer called me to check the cake. Still a bit gushy in the center. Five more minutes should do it. My thoughts turned back to Amy's birthday party. Four little friends for her fourth birthday. Before she started nursery school last fall, she had been a tag-a-long with big sister Jenny. This year, she had friends of her own. And since Amy's birthday fell on Saturday, the party could be on the actual day. Perfect timing. I wanted everything else about it to be perfect, too.

I went down my mental checklist. One more thing to do tonight—wrap her present from Mom and Dad. It seemed too small, but it was all she had asked for: two stuffed mice made of real fur. I had looked in a dozen stores before finding those tiny, realistic-looking treasures. The timer sounded again. This time I removed the cake pans from the oven, wiped the counter, turned out the lights and went upstairs.

In the study, Ralph was watching television. "What's on?" I asked.

"*Quincy,*" he said moving over to make room on the daybed for me.

"Oh," I remarked absently. "I just hafta wrap Amy's present." I didn't like *Quincy*. Too much death and yelling. When I had asked Ralph why he watched it, his answer had been matter-of-fact: because Quincy lives on a sailboat. Sailing was another of Ralph's hobbies. It had grown out of his woodworking when he built a small sailboard-type boat. Like woodworking, he made it a family thing.

I rummaged in the closet for wrapping paper. When Ralph said, "There's his sailboat," I turned to see the picture on the screen. "Pretty neat, huh! Look, he's got everything in there, even a phone." (Mobile phones were not common in 1978)

"Yeah, not bad." I replied with genuine interest. "I guess..." My voice trailed off as I spread wrapping paper on the desk. I had been thinking this week about sailing. About our near-disastrous adventure of the summer before and how my fear had gotten in the way. About Ralph's whimsical wish to someday retire on a sailboat. I had decided I could trust my captain after all, as long as I could stow my sewing machine to use when we were in port. This was not the time to tell him about that decision, though. I would save it for a special romantic moment. Maybe tomorrow night. We were supposed to go out to dinner with friends to an exceptionally fine restaurant. Afterward would be the perfect time to tell him.

I finished wrapping the little mice. The TV show ended. We got ready for bed and made our rounds: Ralph checked the doors and lights; I checked on the girls. The routine was habitual, comfortable. It didn't need conversation. We crawled into bed in companionable silence and nestled like two spoons in a drawer.

Until that moment, I hadn't realized how much emotional and physical energy I was spending on birthday preparations. As I relaxed a bit and the tension began to slip away from my tired body, tears began to flow. "I don't want my baby to be four years old tomorrow," I sobbed, "'cause then she won't be a *baby* any more."

Ralph just held me and let me cry. When I calmed down some he said, "I always wondered if mommies and daddies make love on their daughter's wedding night." He paused. "I think probably the mommies just cry."

I gave a laugh that was half sob and snuggled closer, quieted by his love.

Chapter 3 The Dark, Dark Day

An open window overlooked North Philadelphia, framing wave after wave of tar-black row house roofs. On the crest of each wave rode a line of deteriorating brick facades darkened by city soot. A black water tower on black legs rose out of the middle of this black ocean: a grotesque serpent in a grim sea. The picture seemed ironically appropriate. It matched my dark emotions and the wave-like nausea of my stomach. I was sitting in a shabby fourth-floor waiting room at Temple University Hospital while my husband was undergoing emergency brain surgery. I stared at the view, shivering despite the warmth of the April afternoon.

Two hours earlier I had been in the shining, spring-green and daffodil-yellow suburbs frosting a birthday cake, expecting Ralph home any minute. Then the phone call. A strange doctor on the other end spoke foreign-sounding words. Neural aneurysm.

Unconscious. CAT scan. Neurosurgeon. My anguished, "Oh my God!" still echoed in my ears.

If I closed my eyes to the black rooftops in front of me, the white CAT scan image of the massive blood clot in Ralph's brain floated menacingly into view. The young emergency room intern, sugary and patronizing, had said, "Your husband is very ill." I didn't need anyone to tell me how serious it was. Somehow, I knew he was near death. But he had to live! He just had to be all right! He was my lover, my best friend in the whole world. *Oh God, let him live so we can raise our two little girls together.*

"Do you want to pray?" The question came from our friend Rod, who waited with me through Ralph's surgery.

"I...I don't think I know how," I said, still staring out the window. Was God out there somewhere beyond that ugly, black water tower?

Rod's reply was a question. "Isn't that what we've been doing? But if you feel the need for formal prayer, I'll pray with you."

"No. That's okay. Thanks anyway."

If my fervent wishes, my inner anguish, could be called prayer, then, yes, I had been praying. I doubted it. How could I be praying when I wasn't sure who to pray to? Oh, I believed that God existed, but God was a remote, impersonal, philosophical concept. I pushed theological questions out of my mind, concentrated on the water tower, and tried to will my stomach to stop churning and my hands to stop trembling.

The neurosurgical intensive care unit (NICU) was dimly lighted except for the central nurses' station and the light over Ralph's bed where a nurse was adjusting monitor leads and tubing. The bed was cranked into the sitting position. Ralph's head was swathed in bandages, and he was still asleep. Machines whirred, blipped, and beeped all around him. Everything was white and sterile. I wasn't sure I was allowed to touch him, but I took his hand anyway and held it for a few minutes. It was warm and reassuringly alive. There was still hope. I kissed him on the cheek before I left.

At home, our adopted-grandparent neighbors, Jean and Al, played paper games with Jenny and Amy at the kitchen table. I lay crumpled on the couch, weak and sick and scared. Outside, the bright spring greens and yellows became engulfed in the blackness of night, like the black tar roofs in the city. Rod's wife Bernice hovered over me, sympathetic and attentive. My answers to her questions were perfunctory.

"No, I can't eat anything." "Just some gingerale." "Thank you." "Call our doctor? I don't think there's any need... Oh, for me. Why? No, I don't want any tranquilizers." *I want my husband!*

"Sure. Yes." *Yes call the church prayer chain. I don't care if it's sometimes a gossip chain. Anything that might help bring back my husband.*

A little later, our minister, Jim Bell, held my hand, and I held my little girls close, and we were all linked to everyone else in the room as he prayed a pastoral sort of prayer. *Where did all these people come from?* "...And Lord, we ask you for Ralph's complete healing... " *Yes, yes.*

"No, I really can't eat a thing." *I suppose I'll have to eat again sometime. Maybe she's right. Maybe some Valium could help calm my stomach enough to keep food down.* "Okay," I said weakly. "Doctor B's number is by the phone in the kitchen."

The tiny yellow pill looked harmless, actually impotent. Doubtfully, I placed it on my tongue and washed it down with a swallow of gingerale.

When I awoke, the sun was streaming in the east window of the bedroom, and birds were singing merrily. I still felt tired, and I had a strange sense of having had the worst nightmare of my life, though I could not remember what it was about. I reached for the reassuring comfort of the warm body next to me. My hand rested on cool sheet. Suddenly, I was wide-awake as the events of the day before flooded my mind. My stomach resumed its churning.

Bernice was talking to someone on the patio from the window of the back bedroom/study. "What time is it? Oh dear, we completely forgot about changing the clocks. No. You go on. Come back after church. You did? I don't know."

I steadied my wobbly legs by holding onto a doorframe as I slipped into the bathroom. Jenny and Amy were stirring, asking questions in little girl voices. Bernice had already gone to them when I emerged from the bathroom and crossed the hall to their room. They were my children. Mine and Ralph's. They were here. They were real. I wanted to hold them and comfort them and be comforted by them.

"Can Daddy come home today?"

"No, he had a pretty serious operation. He'll have to stay in the hospital for a while."

"How long?"

"I don't know."

Over the two blonde heads, I caught Bernice's eye as she sat on the other bed. "Rod already called the hospital. They said there's no change."

"I need to get down there," I said. "I want to be there when he wakes up." The day had purpose. I had to get through it. I had to have strength. I had to eat something. I took another little yellow pill before I washed my face.

Chapter 4 Darkness Lingers

In the days and weeks that followed, Ralph remained in a deep coma. Neighbors and friends brought food and offered babysitting and rides to the hospital so I could spend as much time with Ralph as possible. While he was in intensive care, I could see him only for brief periods, so I spent the time between visits in the fourth-floor waiting room. The black view from the window became familiar—no less ominous, just familiar.

I read everything I could find on brain injuries, brain function, and coma. I planned what I would tell Ralph when I could see him again. When I ran out of other things to think about, I cautiously approached the questions I had avoided the first day: Why did this happen to Ralph? Why us? Why anybody? Where are you God?

Mr. Bell became a daily part of our lives, visiting with Ralph and with me, driving me to the hospital, praying for us, encouraging. I felt he understood. He had been through brain surgery himself when he was about Ralph's age. His had been to remove a tumor, which left him blind in one eye and with a small depression in his forehead.

At home in the evenings, I talked with the girls about Daddy and we cried together. Jenny, age six, seemed to understand much of what was going on. She missed her "buddy" terribly. Amy I worried about because she did not express her feelings as openly as Jenny. Crepe paper streamers still hung from the dining room chandelier weeks after her party. It had gone on as planned with Jean, Al and Bernice filling in for Ralph and me. I had not given Amy her present from Mommy and Daddy yet. She hadn't asked about it, and I waited for the day when Ralph and I could give it to her together.

After the girls were in bed, I missed Ralph most acutely. That's when we would have shared a snack at the kitchen table and talked about our day, our plans, our feelings. To avoid the loneliness, I got ready for bed with the girls. After tucking them in, I quickly fell asleep from nervous exhaustion. Then I would wake before dawn, find myself alone in the bed, and remember our living nightmare. The nervousness would resume. I could not get warm. My stomach churned. I would get up and take a Valium so I could begin the day. I depended on those little pills and worried about possible addiction.

Only when I walked into Ralph's hospital room and saw that he was still alive could I calm down. I would stay with him as long as they let me, hold his hand, talk to him, play tapes the girls had made for him, adjust the pillows to make him more comfortable. I had read about coma patients remembering things that had happened while they were comatose, so I kept talking as if he really could hear.

I rapidly lost weight. I was grateful for the people who did housework, yard work and babysitting, brought meals, and drove me to the hospital forty-minutes into the city. The first two weeks, I was too shaky to drive at all, not even to take my turn in the nursery school carpool or go to the supermarket a mile away.

Ralph's brothers and mother came from Pittsburgh three weeks after his surgery. With them along for moral support, I drove to the hospital for the first time. I hoped Ed and Bruce could jolt Ralph out of his coma. They could not.

The following week, my parents made the same 300-mile trip across the state. I cried long and hard like a hurt child when they got here. They helped by taking care of the girls and managing things at home, giving me more time with Ralph.

Our pastor Mr. Bell often served as my personal chauffeur on the daily commute to the city, even after I began driving again. More than that, he would stay to visit with both of us, pitch in to help me with the nursing care I was learning to do for Ralph, pray for us and always encourage us. We saw him every day for the first month or so, at least four or five days a week for the entire nine months Ralph was at Temple Hospital. On days when he did not drive me, he would visit at the hospital while I was there. Like the Good Shepherd in Jesus' parable, he left the rest of the sheep to tend to the one missing from the flock.

Other people also offered rides, which I gladly accepted, especially on weekdays when traffic was heavy and parking was difficult. Sometimes it was a retiree from church, or a friend who had the afternoon off, or somebody's cousin who worked second shift in the city. I've forgotten many of their names. Some have long ago gone to be with the Lord. I appreciated each one of them.

One day our friend Rich went with me. Rich had been a student minister at our church the year before. He and Ralph had worked with the youth fellowship and become good friends. I knew they had had some deep theological discussions. On the way home Rich said, "In that room with Ralph, I had a definite sense of the presence of God."

"You did?" I asked. "I know I sense the presence of Ralph there, but I don't know about God. If God is there, why doesn't he do something? Why is Ralph still in a coma?"

"I don't know," Rich answered, "but God is there. He's taking care of Ralph."

"I wonder if Ralph knows that. He had lots of questions about God."

"Yes," Rich agreed, "but they were the kind of questions that come from faith."

Was Ralph being sustained by his faith? It was comforting to think he might be. How did Rich know God was there with Ralph? I wanted some awareness and assurance myself. I could no longer ignore the haunting questions about God.

Chapter 5 Grieving

Two or three weeks into Ralph's hospitalization, when he was still in intensive care and listed in critical condition, a well-meaning friend quoted Romans 8:28 to me. Rather, she misquoted it. Recited incompletely and out of context the verse implies that God maliciously causes bad things because they are good for us—like some bitter medicine. If I had had a large Bible handy, I would have thrown it at that woman. There could be no good in the tragedy that had come upon our family, and if God caused it, I wanted no part of him!

When I hear of Christians persevering with unwavering faith through incredible trials, I can't help but view the stories with skepticism. I have no doubt that their faith is genuine, but I wonder if they truly remember what they were feeling and thinking during their crisis. It is much easier to forget.

I know I was confused about what I believed because I wrote my thoughts in an ongoing letter to Ralph. Over the months when he was comatose or semi-comatose, that letter filled 33 pages of unlined 8½ by 11 inch paper with small handwriting and no margins. My hope was that someday Ralph would be able to read the letter and we could discuss the questions I posed in it. We had always discussed such things before his brain injury.

Over time, I have come to know that Christianity stands up to any intellectual questions I can ask about it. Then, I was not asking intellectual questions; I was just feeling, and my feelings affected my faith.

- First, there was FEAR—profound heart-pounding, hands-sweating, knees-buckling, gut-wrenching fear.
- Then there was PAIN—the deep, heart pain of watching a loved one suffer and being unable to relieve his physical torture.
- I began to WORRY about details and consequences. *Are they keeping a pillow between his knees? What if he dies? Is he getting enough liquids? What will happen to me? Is he sleeping? What will happen to our children?*
- FRUSTRATION set in. I felt put-down and powerless when dealing with medical professionals. Individuals seemed caring,

but the bureaucracy of hospital organization seemed to slow responsiveness to patient needs short of a life-or-death crisis. *If they can't fix the brain, why don't they at least relieve the pain?*

- ANGER, RESENTMENT, and BITTERNESS followed. At first, these were directed at people whose perceived inattentiveness had aggravated the worrisome problems. Eventually negative feelings shifted to the system, the injury and God. *How can you leave him in obvious agony? You made him, God; why won't you fix him?*
- A general feeling of OPPRESSION set in. God seemed far, far away.

The crisis dragged on for weeks and months with no real progress and numerous setbacks. The intense emotions became chronic GRIEF, DEPRESSION, and HOPELESSNESS. I grieved for the losses, my own and Ralph's—lost function, lost relationship, lost love, lost security. I went through the classic stages of bereavement: shock, denial, isolation, anger, bargaining, depression, and eventual acceptance.

My 33-page letter to Ralph was part of the grieving process. Looking over it, I can see the various stages. I was already past the initial shock, but denial is apparent when I talk about my hopes for Ralph's recovery. (Some of the denial was due to my naivete about brain injuries.) Isolation and loneliness are recurrent. Anger is expressed frequently. A pivotal event in the letter is the depression that ensued when I began to realize the extent and permanency of Ralph's brain injury. The entire letter is, in a sense, bargaining with God; if I could only figure out God, maybe Ralph could be healed. At the end, I see the beginnings of acceptance.

Early in the letter, I relate how, during my visits with Ralph, I tried to encourage him. I told him I loved him, that he was going to get well, that he would have to learn to do many things all over again, but there was no reason why he could not make a full recovery. Then follows my statement of faith as it was at the time.

"I've trusted in love—your love for me, Jenny, Amy, life, and my love and the love of your friends for you—to give you the will to live and to come back to consciousness. I've trusted in your own spirit, the 'ground of your being,' to give you the determination and strength to overcome whatever handicaps you might have, to relearn what you need to [in order] to make a complete recovery. I've trusted that time, nature, medical science, and a lot of love would get us through this mess and see us back together. You'd have to say I've been trusting in God as my concept of God has been—a kind of combination of nature, love, and the knowledge that is the basis of modern medicine. At the same time, I've felt we would have to work very hard to make this miracle happen."

My letter goes on to tell of ways that I tried to stimulate Ralph's senses and the struggle to get hospital staff to do more therapy. I tell about the friends who were visiting and learning to give him additional physical therapy. Then, I encourage him to "keep trying no matter how difficult or frustrating things seem." I can only imagine the level of frustration Ralph must have felt. For him, merely opening his eyes seems to have been as difficult as running a triathlon would be for an untrained but healthy individual.

Our faithful pastor was the first to find a concrete sign that Ralph was regaining consciousness. We were both there that day on either side of the bed. Mr. Bell was telling Ralph, "Try real hard to open your eyes, son. You can do it." With two fingers, he lifted Ralph's eyelids saying, "Look at Nancy." The eyes slowly moved in my direction.

"Hey, he did it!" I said. Then to Ralph, "Can you look back at Jim?" The eyes moved back. Excited, I took over holding Ralph's eyelids open and commanded him to look at me. Again, his eyes turned in my direction. He knew! He understood!

After that, I increased my efforts to communicate with Ralph, to stimulate, entertain, and encourage him. A couple of months after his surgery, he was tracking with his eyes consistently when someone held them open and holding them about halfway open by himself for brief periods. Sometimes he was also able to give a weak hand squeeze on command. I was encouraged. However, the hospital staff did not seem to see what Mr. Bell and I saw or share my hope.

Then there was another crisis. Ralph had been having episodes of sweating and unexplained fever. At those times, the nurses would put him on a refrigerated pad to lower his body temperature. Eleven weeks into his hospitalization, a nurse left him on the cooling pad too long, inducing hypothermia. He lapsed into deep coma for almost twenty-four hours. When he started responding again, hospital staff finally took notice.

Ralph's case was assigned to a new neurosurgery resident, Dr. Smythe, who ordered more therapies. Physical and occupational therapists began taking him to the PT gym each day. Psychologists and speech therapists began charting his responses for consistency and trying to establish communication.

The psychologist arranged for Ralph to see Jenny and Amy once a week in her office. I tried to prepare the girls ahead of time, telling them what Daddy would look like, what he could and could not do, about the wheelchair and other equipment. The psychologist also talked with them. We made the first visit a mini-birthday party and gave Amy her long overdue present from Mom and Dad—the little fur mice.

Dr. Smythe talked to me one day about the prognosis. He spoke in positive terms of feeding devices, communication boards, and electric wheelchairs operated by blowing on switches. I plied the same questions I had been asking for nearly three months. "What is he going to be able to do? How long will it take?"

This young resident gave the most direct and honest answer any doctor had yet given. He simply said, "I don't know." Then he added, "For a person coming out of a coma, if Ralph were going to get back much function he should be doing more moving around at this point."

It was not until after Dr. Smythe left the room that the implication of what he was saying began to sink into my mind. *Ralph would be an invalid for the rest of his life.* Over the next two days, I wrestled with this information alone while I tried to figure out how I would tell Jenny and Amy what lay ahead for us. I would have to tell them that Daddy would not be home for a long, long time and that he would probably be in a wheelchair and not able to do much when he did come home.

In my letter, I told Ralph, "I wasn't scared anymore, at least not like the gripping panic of the first few days, but deep depression set in. I could not even force a smile to comfort you. You must have felt my mood, honey. During that time, you had more of those awful sweats, even though you had no fever. To me, their apparent cause seemed to be frustration and discomfort, and I saw fear and panic in your eyes whenever I found you that way." We needed a miracle, but my god of love, nature, knowledge, and hard work was not bringing one about.

The topic of miracles often came up in conversations with friends. We were all hoping for one. Some believed miracles happen slowly and need lots of work. Some believed they happen suddenly. Some thought the miracle was that Ralph was able to get medical treatment that would not have been available five years earlier. CAT scan imaging, which guided the surgeon to remove the clot from his brain, was new then. Bernice thought the love Ralph and I had for each other was the miracle. One person, however, kept telling me of a different kind of miracle.

Chapter 6 A Candle in the Gloom

When I answered the doorbell one morning about four weeks into Ralph's hospitalization, Marty stood on our front porch with a bunch of homegrown daisies in her hand, a hint of shyness in her smile. "These are for you," she said.

If her offering seemed a little awkward, my response was more so; I still could not get used to being on the receiving end of such gestures of kindness and sympathy. I recited the customary, "Thank you." Then I added, "maybe Ralph will be able to enjoy them now that he's been moved from intensive care." (Flowers had not been permitted in ICU.)

"Oh, no," Marty said. "They're for *you*. You enjoy them here at home."

"Oh," I said weakly. I had not rehearsed a response for that one. So far all the cards and flowers had been for Ralph. The casseroles had been for the girls and me, though I felt so little like eating that they might as well have been bunches of daisies, too. I fumbled for a few appropriate phrases.

Marty went on. She apologized for not coming over sooner. I wondered why. I had not been expecting her. I didn't even know her that well. Then she said, "My Bible study group has been praying for Ralph. I'm sure God is working in his life and he's going to be all right." She seemed so certain, the shy awkwardness suddenly gone.

It was the first positive forecast I had heard. I wanted to believe her but was afraid to. The situation looked bleak. Ralph seemed to be out of immediate danger of dying, but he was still in a deep coma. I had been told that the longer he remained in this state, the more serious and irreversible the brain damage. I sensed it had already been too long. There had been a subtle change in the way the hospital staff gave his prognosis; they no longer talked about *when* he regains consciousness but *IF*.

Here was Marty telling me Ralph would be "all right," reawakening hope beneath the curse of *IF*. When she turned to go to her car, she promised to come by again. I went back in the house with the bunch of daisies in my hand, wondering. Did I dare to think that Ralph would not only live, but also be all right?

I was not all right myself. With my husband and best friend in the hospital, my constant companion was a nervous upset stomach. I continued to lose weight. I went about the work of daily living mechanically, having neither the will nor the strength to do more than was necessary. I depended on other people and those little yellow Valium pills. I must have looked haggard; when I walked into Ralph's hospital room, the morning after he was moved from intensive care, a nurse had asked if he was my son.

The tasks that were most taxing were the ones Ralph usually did—winding the clocks, lugging heavy trashcans to the street, paying bills. The activities most painful were the ones we had done together, such as tucking the girls in at night or going to church. Oddly, I felt least upset when I was with Ralph at the hospital. After Marty left, I was anxious to go to him and share her glimmer of hope. It seemed a bit easier to get lunch for the girls that day, and take them to a sitter.

The spark of optimism, however, was too small to overcome the big, oppressive *IF*. Over the weeks that followed, Ralph's condition remained critical. He received oxygen through a tube in his throat, antibiotics through a tube in his arm, and food through a tube in his stomach. He was rigid and spastic most of the time. Muscles atrophied and tendons shortened despite passive physical therapy. He was gaunt and pallid. As his body degenerated, so did my spirits. There was still the hopeful sign that he could follow with his eyes when we held the lids open, but I could not convince doctors to try it. It was not one of their standard tests, and they continued to offer little encouragement.

Encouragement waned at home, also. Cards and letters were less frequent. The casseroles stopped coming, and fewer rides were offered. There still seemed to be a supply of caring babysitters, but I had to ask and make the arrangements. I was glad to be more independent, doing more housework and driving, but at the same time, I felt abandoned.

When helpers began drifting away, Marty came again. Her visits got more regular as others became irregular. Always she brought something for me, such as a bouquet of flowers or a plate of homemade cookies. Always she said that her Bible study group was praying for us and she was sure Ralph was going to be all right. Gradually she went on to tell me more about healing in the Bible, and about how Jesus came to bring healing, not only to people two thousand years ago, but also to us today. I listened feeling somewhat uneasy and wondered if this group was, well, a little kooky.

After a few visits, I was convinced Marty must have gotten in with a bunch of crazies in that Bible study group. We belonged to the same Presbyterian church. Ralph and her husband John, both rational electrical engineers, had served together as elders. We never heard any of this stuff about healing in our church. But then, Mr. Bell did continue to pray for Ralph to be completely healed. I was confused.

I longed for Ralph's honest opinion and advice. In my letter to him, I related what Marty was telling me and expressed my doubts. "You know the trouble I've had accepting literally many of the biblical writings about Jesus: the virgin birth, the miracles, and the resurrection. To me, the important thing about the miracles was not whether they actually happened, but that they showed people are worth caring for, and the resurrection was probably a spiritual or psychological one rather than a physical one. The only magic spirit in my life has been your love. I know that because, whenever we've had a fight and you are mad at me, I live in hell until we make up. Is it surprising that my god has come to be defined by the things I see working in my life: love like yours and ours, the wonders of nature, honesty, truth, knowledge, a searching mind, tolerance, peace, concern for others? I just can't swallow all Marty is telling me."

Ralph's physical problems seemed beyond the power of nature to heal, and the virtues I held in such high esteem were not helping. We needed the Jesus type of healing power Marty talked about. My latest attempts to reach God did not seem to be getting through, any more than did my anguished silent groaning in that drab waiting room during Ralph's brain surgery.

About that time we got a letter from Tom, Ralph's best friend from high school. He and his wife Jeanette and their two children were moving from Colorado to Washington D.C. for the coming year. I had not had the heart to contact him yet with our awful news, but I had to write back. (Before email and the breakup of AT&T, we actually communicated by hand-written letters.) Tom called as soon as they got to Washington, and they came up to Philadelphia the next weekend.

Tom and Jeanette both went with me to the hospital, and spent time helping to make Ralph comfortable, talking to him, watching and waiting for his smallest responses. While other people were backing off, unable to handle their own emotional reactions to Ralph's gross condition, Tom and Jeanette remained supportive. They came to visit about once a month for the entire year they lived that close.

On one of their trips, the three of us were standing around Ralph's bed when a little elderly lady came over and asked about him. I thought she was visiting his roommate and simply showing polite concern. (Later, I learned the family of the roommate did not know her either. We never found out who she was, where she came from, or why she was there.) She asked if she could pray for Ralph, and I said okay. Our whole church was praying for him. So was Marty's Bible study group, and I had certainly tried. It couldn't hurt to add one more.

The woman took a small vial of liquid from her purse and started to open it. *Was she going to give him some quack medicine?* She saw the questioning look on my face and quickly explained, "Oil. I'll just put a drop on his forehead." She dabbed the oil on her fingers and touched them to Ralph's forehead as she prayed aloud.

Her prayer was like none I had ever heard before. It was no sedate, formal petition addressed to "Heavenly Father" or "Dear God." She talked to *Jesus* as if she knew him personally. She poured out our pathetic situation with great emotion, asking Jesus to bring him out of the coma. At one point, she began to tremble and seemed to be on the verge of tears. When she finished, she confidently told us Ralph would get better. "You'll see a difference soon," she promised. *Could this impassioned prayer to Jesus be the kind that worked?*

Gradually, Ralph became able to hold his eyes open by himself for short periods, but his body continued to deteriorate. I became more frustrated and depressed. One day, when Marty came to the house, her hopefulness contrasted so sharply with my dark mood that I broke down and sobbed. I told Marty I wanted to go to the Bible study with her. I hoped I could find something there that would help Ralph.

To my relief, the ladies at the Bible study did not seem like kooks. They were normal suburban homemakers from churches of several mainstream denominations, including Presbyterian. The teacher, Peg, was a warm, soft-spoken lady, a registered nurse. Her lesson seemed thoroughly researched, and she had a low-key, logical presentation. The scientist in me liked that.

We arrived as the lesson was beginning, so Marty did not take time to introduce me beforehand. I just listened quietly. At the end, several of the ladies prayed aloud for various needs of others. Peg concluded by praying for Ralph and for me. I started crying. I hated being so out-of-control over my emotions, but everyone was very kind and understanding. Afterward, I couldn't wait to get to the hospital to tell Ralph about the Bible study and see if there was any improvement.

That afternoon, the student nurses helped get Ralph into a high-backed chair, propping him with pillows and rolled blankets. He seemed more alert when sitting up. That was when he was most likely to be able to respond in some way. I had discovered that he could sometimes follow commands to blink his eyes, or squeeze with his right hand. With the tracheotomy tube in his throat, he could not talk, but if I covered the tube briefly with my thumb, sending air through his larynx, he would give an audible moan. I told him about the Bible study that morning, watching closely for any sign of reaction.

The internal medicine specialist came by on his rounds. He was the doctor in charge of Ralph's general medical care. An older man with a kindly manner, he actually spoke *to* Ralph. What a contrast he was to the neurosurgeons, who came in a group with their students and stood around the bed talking *about* Ralph in technical terms.

The internist took Ralph's blood pressure, listened to his heart and lungs, and looked him over, top to toe. Putting his hand into Ralph's he asked, "Can you squeeze my hand, Ralph?" Ralph squeezed. "Good!" said the doctor, surprise and pleasure apparent in his voice. "Can you blink your eyes for me?" Ralph blinked slowly. "That's it. Can you blink again?" Ralph did. "Very good!" said the doctor, smiling. His entry on Ralph's chart for that day was scrawled across the page in great big letters: PATIENT RESPONDING. NO LONGER COMATOSE.

I was elated. Maybe now those pompous neurosurgeons would believe that Ralph was aware. They seemed to dismiss my reports as the wishful thinking of a distraught and irrational wife. Surely, they could not ignore the objective statement of another physician. The student nurses who had witnessed the doctor's visit were smiling. When Jim Bell stopped in later and heard the news, he was also encouraged.

Ralph seemed tense, a little agitated or uncomfortable. I put my thumb over his trachea tube as I asked, "What is it? Can you say something?" His reply sounded like a very bad amateur ventriloquist: "I lu yo." I grinned for the first time since our nightmare had begun. "I love you, too," I whispered.

Mr. Bell choked back tears as he took our hands for his customary prayer. I was glad he was there to witness this milestone; he had been praying for it. As we left the hospital, I told him, "Ralph is going to make it. I'm sure of it, now."

Had something in the prayers of the Bible study ladies finally made the difference? The teacher's prayer was similar to that of the little lady who had anointed Ralph with oil, though minus the emotional fervor. Peg's manner was much quieter with no trembling or tears, but both women had talked to Jesus as if they knew him personally.

The next Tuesday, I went back to the Bible study with hope and many questions. As I listened each week, I began to see the Bible in a new way. It was not just an ethical guidebook and collection of stories from long ago, but God speaking to people today. Peg said that the things God promised to ancient people— guidance, salvation, healing—he also gives to us today. The key to receiving these blessings seemed to be Jesus, but why and how?

Peg was very patient with my questions. Never did she tell me to "just believe." She always answered me logically. She showed me many Old Testament prophecies fulfilled by Jesus, and she loaned me books about the historical "proofs" I sought. I was surprised to learn that there is so much scholarly evidence to support the accuracy of the ancient biblical manuscripts and the validity of the stories.

The lives of the Apostles after Jesus' death and resurrection impressed me. Ancient historians corroborate the New Testament accounts in the Book of Acts, and go on to tell how the Apostles died. Most of them suffered a martyr's death. Could anyone speak that boldly or endure such hardship and opposition if he were not absolutely convinced that what he had witnessed about Jesus was true?

In the early church, the Apostles performed miraculous healings in Jesus' name. The Bible study ladies told of receiving healings in Jesus' name, also. Some happened at special prayer services. Others came gradually when the women prayed by themselves or with a friend or family member. None of their modern day miracles was as dramatic as the one I longed to see for Ralph, but their accounts seemed truthful.

The stories that impressed me most were the ones where the women told about the Holy Spirit giving them strength and wisdom to cope with a difficult situation. They had been through financial troubles and natural disasters, broken family relationships and teenage children in rebellion. Especially moving was Peg's story of being attacked and raped in a stairwell at the hospital where she worked. As she recovered physically, Jesus healed her emotional wounds and freed her from fear. How, I

wondered, does one get to know Jesus that way?

Chapter 7 A Kindred Heart

Once Ralph was out of intensive care, I only went back to the drab and dreary waiting room on brief occasions while he was being taken for x-rays or tests. The view from the window remained bleak. The people I saw there looked as I had felt: fearful, nervous, and bereft. When it was time for their short visits to ICU, they went stiffly, anxiously. When they came back, their faces reflected their fear or hope. They worked out anxieties in different ways. Some smoked; some ate candy or drank coffee and sodas; some cried; some sat in stony silence.

In July, I noticed one couple that was different. They appeared to be in their forties, a tall man and woman with friendly faces. His had the wrinkles around the eyes that come from laughter. Hers, framed by short blond hair, had a serene smile. A reassuring peace seemed to emanate from them, and the others in the room leaned on them. He would go to put coins in a parking meter for someone. She would offer a word of encouragement. Together, they even brought a few smiles to the morose expressions of the others. I wondered how they could be so tranquil in this awful place.

The next time I saw them, I happened to sit near them, and the woman introduced herself. Her name was also Nancy. Her husband was Hank.

"Do you have someone in intensive care?" I asked.

"Yes, our son, Fred. He was in an auto accident," she replied.

"How's he doing?"

"Not very well. He's in a coma." Her expression remained serene.

"Oh, I'm sorry," I mumbled.

"Who are you visiting?" she asked.

I told her a little about my husband, then went back to the book I had brought to read. I was relieved that she didn't attempt further conversation.

The next time I saw Nancy and Hank was on a Sunday afternoon. Tom and Jeanette had come from D.C. for the weekend and accompanied me to the hospital. Together we got Ralph into a reclining wheelchair and took him to the waiting room for a change of scene. The windows were open to a warm summer breeze. We pulled chairs around Ralph, hoping he would be stimulated and encouraged by our light conversation. Nancy and Hank were the only other people in the room. We did not converse with them except for a polite greeting, but I was aware of their presence. Nancy's smile, whenever I glanced her way spoke encouragement. That curious peacefulness surrounded them.

Not long after that, Fred was moved into the room across the hall from Ralph. His mother sat at his bedside constantly. As I would come and go, she would wave to me and smile. She looked so happy I thought Fred must be much better, so I asked the nurses about him. They said Fred was stable but still deeply comatose and suffering the effects of many injuries besides the head injury. He was spastic and rigid, showing no sign of conscious brain function. In short, he was in much worse shape than Ralph had ever been. Nobody held much hope for Fred to recover. So why did his mother look so happy? It didn't make sense.

One Saturday afternoon as I was leaving Ralph's room, I caught Nancy's eye and her wave as usual. My curiosity got the best of me. I hesitated just a moment, then stepped across the hall into Fred's room.

"Hi. How are you? How's Fred, today?"

"I'm fine. Freddy, meet Nancy. Her husband's in the room across the hall and she stopped to say hello to us." She spoke to Fred as if he understood, just as I tried to do with Ralph.

I moved toward the head of the bed where I would be in Fred's line of vision if he could actually see me. The nurses had not exaggerated. Fred looked awful; several teeth missing, ugly scars everywhere, head turned spastically to one side with eyes open, but unresponsive. Nancy gave me a progress report, speaking positively about how his many wounds were healing and about his eventual recovery. She seemed realistically aware of all that was wrong with him. She should be; she spent much of her time helping with his nursing care. Why, I wondered, was she so optimistic?

Nancy seemed to sense my question before I could ask. "Because," she said, "God doesn't want Fred, or Ralph, to be like this. I know that one day Fred is going to be healed, whether here or there." She gestured toward heaven.

I didn't know how to respond and couldn't anyway—not with the lump in my throat. Fortunately, I didn't have to. Jim Bell, who had stopped at the hospital to take me home, came looking for me and stepped into the room as Nancy was speaking. He picked up the conversation for both of us, and asked Nancy if he could quote her in his sermon the next day. She said, "Of course," with a little laugh. All the way home, and for several days afterward, I mulled over what she had said.

God doesn't want Ralph to be like this? I wanted to believe that, but the evidence was denying it. He had made so little progress and had so very far to go. Meanwhile, his suffering was intense. He was emaciated despite surgery to insert a feeding tube in his stomach. His tracheotomy tube caused constant irritation and mucous in his airways. He continued to have unexplained fever. He had a raging skin infection on his back, which doctors seemed unable to diagnose. When moving him, the staff often scraped his back on the bed frame or wheelchair, adding abrasions and gashes to his already raw skin.

Ralph would often become extremely rigid, panting from the physical exertion of his tension. He would break out in sweating so profuse he looked like someone had thrown a bucket of water on him. At those times, the expression on his face showed pain, fear, and panic. Whenever I found him in a panicky sweat, he was lying on his right side, which had a large, ulcerating pressure sore on the hip. As soon as I moved him to any other position, he calmed down. I asked the nurses not to put him on his right side, since he was obviously uncomfortable that way. Nevertheless, they insisted he had to be in that positioning half the time. The sore on his hip continued to grow, adding to his discomfort and frustration.

God, if you don't want Ralph to be like this, why don't you do something about it? Something, at least, to relieve his suffering and pain? I didn't know what God wanted for Ralph, but I knew I wanted him well. And I wanted it "here," not "there."

Though I could not embrace Nancy's calm acceptance of God's will, "here or there," I was drawn to her serenity. Our conversations became frequent and longer. We exchanged notes on the practical details of caring for our two patients. We were both amazed that, in a hospital with a neurosurgery reputation, the staff seemed so inexperienced with comatose patients—as if Ralph and Fred were the first ones they had ever seen. Indeed, for those who had the most patient contact, the nursing students and resident doctors, Ralph and Fred probably were their first such cases.

Youth and inexperience aren't always a bad thing. Nancy and I found our greatest ally in a young, enthusiastic occupational therapist. She answered many of our questions about neurological function, which the surgeons couldn't or wouldn't answer. She took time to look through the medical literature for suggestions on handling similar patients. She listened to our ideas, also, and helped us try them; for example, positioning a pillow a certain way under a knee or beside a head, or not tucking the top sheet in at the bottom to avoid irritating toes. When we found a technique that worked, our OT friend helped us persuade the nursing staff to use it.

During one of our talks, I asked Nancy if she believed in miracles. She said she did and she was certainly praying for one for Ralph as well as for Fred. I felt a twinge of guilt. I hadn't thought much about praying for Fred. I wasn't sure God was hearing my prayers for Ralph.

While I was seeking a big, dramatic miracle, Nancy was quietly praying about little steps. Each day she asked what we needed—a restful night, a break in the fever, healing of the rash, lessening of the rigidity—and said she would pray about those things for us. Slowly, those problems began to subside, though I could not trace any of the changes to a specific day or prayer. I began to wish I could know the peacefulness with which this kindred heart persevered in praying all of us through each day's difficulties.

Meanwhile, I continued going with Marty to the Bible study on Tuesday mornings. Each week, the ladies prayed for Ralph, and I saw small improvements. The hospital staff seemed to be taking more interest in him, filling his days with therapies. I spent much of my visiting time learning the routines and helping with them.

I was so busy looking for changes in Ralph that I hardly noticed some changes taking place in me. I was finding it a little easier to face each day and becoming less dependent on the Valium, except in the early morning. I was doing more housework and driving myself to the hospital more often. I even drove Ralph's TR6 one Sunday—stick shift in city traffic with a stop light at every intersection—and then walked into his room grinning to say, "Guess how I got here today!" Did Jesus have something to do with my improved emotional state?

When I was alone with Ralph, there wasn't enough time to share all I was learning about the Bible or all of my questions. I wanted to know his thoughts. In my rambling letter, I wrote, "I've got to talk with you, Ralph. You're the only person I know who is honest enough to help me work this thing out rationally without pressure or condemnation. But then, what does it matter what I think or believe? It may be what you believe that's important in the long run."

I had no problem with God as creator. My college physiology courses had convinced me that the intricate biochemical workings of living cells are no accident; life processes have to be directed by a supreme creative power. In addition, I could accept the existence of a God-presence or Holy Spirit. Analogous to radio waves, it enables people to relate to God on a personal level. Jesus was the part of the Trinity that did not make sense. Was he really God in human form? Why was he necessary? How did he fit into my life and problems? Could the man/God who worked miracles 2000 years ago heal Ralph?

We arranged some signals with hand squeezes and eye blinks so Ralph could respond to my yes/no and multiple-choice questions. In this way, he was able to let me know that he thought what I was hearing about Jesus made sense and that he wanted to know more. It was not much of a substitute for real conversation, but it would have to do.

It seemed more than coincidental that improvement in both Ralph's condition and my emotional state had begun when I started going to the Bible study. In early September, with the horrible rash on Ralph's back worse than ever, I decided to put prayer to the test one weekend. I asked for healing of the rash, visualizing dramatic instant improvement. Monday, there was no difference. Tuesday, I asked the ladies in the class to pray for Ralph's back. They did along with the usual prayer for total healing, asking God to "raise him up out of the bed and cause him to move and speak." Well, he moved all right. He had a grand mal seizure that afternoon. For the rest of the week, he was more lethargic and less responsive than he had been in a month. His back was still raw, and by Friday, he had a fever again.

Doubts overshadowed my budding faith. This healing stuff could not be true. Something else the women in the group talked about bothered me. They called it the baptism of the Holy Spirit, and they said anyone who received it could speak in tongues. I had not heard them actually speak in tongues, but they seemed to accept the practice as common. It sounded weird and irrational to me.

I talked with our friends Rich and Carolyn about my reservations. They had been involved in a similar "Charismatic" group when they were in college. Rich, who was studying for the ministry in a conservative denomination, said there was much truth in the teaching I was hearing, but I should be careful. First, of course, the miracles don't always happen. No matter how much faith we have, we are still subject to human sufferings and tragedy. There are no magic formulas for getting prayers answered. Yet, Rich and Carolyn both said they still believed in miracles.

Marty and John had been going to the hospital to work with Ralph in the evenings when I needed to be home with the children. Marty also shared some of my reservations about healing, because she shared my disappointment with Ralph's slow progress and many setbacks. She, too, still believed healing was possible and steadfastly believed in Jesus.

Other Christians continued to encourage. Nancy was praying for daily needs. Pastor Bell faithfully gave practical support. Several people from church volunteered to visit Ralph in the evenings. Church members kept providing childcare after the community babysitting co-op we belonged to dumped us. However, human kindness does not instill faith. God does. His Word in the Bible, his Holy Spirit, and Jesus are the keys to receiving it. This I was only beginning to learn.

Chapter 8 "As the Deer Pants for Streams of Water"

Looking back, I can see that God's Word was powerful. Simply by hearing it in conversations with friends like Nancy, Marty, Rich and Carolyn, the Spirit of God began to instill faith. The Bible itself explains what happened to me.

"Consequently, faith comes from hearing the message, and the message is heard through the word of Christ" (Romans 10:17). Hearing the words of Christ quoted from Scripture and hearing what the Bible says about Christ, the Holy Spirit began to work in my spirit.

"For the word of God is living and active. Sharper than any double-edged sword, it penetrates even to dividing soul and spirit, joints and marrow; it judges the thoughts and attitudes of the heart" (Hebrews 4:12). The living, active words of God touched my heart more deeply than mere human words. They drew me to

God because of his love for me. "For God so loved the world that he gave his one and only Son, that whoever believes in him shall not perish but have eternal life" (John 3:16).

We cannot love or believe in someone we do not know. I spent five years getting to know Ralph and building a friendship before I loved and trusted in him. The initiative was Ralph's; He was the one who called to talk or propose a date. Getting to know and love God was a similar process. God attracted me to himself through words of Scripture that touched my heart. As Jesus says, "No one can come to me unless the Father who sent me draws him" (John 6:44).

The passages that began to draw me to Jesus were ones that hit home by describing feelings or events I experienced. Romans 8:26 explained what happened during the anguishing hours of Ralph's brain surgery: "The Spirit helps us in our weakness. We do not know what we ought to pray for, but the Spirit himself intercedes for us with groans that words cannot express." Rod had asked if I wanted him to pray with me. When I said I didn't know how, he replied, "Isn't that what we've been doing?" Perhaps God heard my inexpressible groaning that day after all.

In Psalms, I discovered laments that echoed mine and probably Ralph's. "I am worn out from groaning; all night long I flood my bed with weeping and drench my couch with tears" (Psalm 6:6). "Why, O Lord, do you reject me and hide your face from me? Your wrath has swept over me; your terrors have destroyed me. All day long they surround me like a flood; they have completely engulfed me. You have taken my companions and loved ones from me; the darkness is my closest friend" (Psalm 88:14, 16-18).

Out of my need, I was searching for God. Psalm 42:1 expresses my longing: "As the deer pants for streams of water, so my soul pants for you, O God."

The Bible instructs us to pray over the sick for their healing. "Is any one of you sick? He should call the elders of the church to pray over him and anoint him with oil in the name of the Lord" (James 5:14). The little lady who prayed over Ralph so passionately had anointed him with oil.

Feeding on the Word, my emotional state began to improve. "Man does not live on bread alone, but on every word that comes from the mouth of God" (Matthew 4:4, Deuteronomy 8:3). The Word of God was the only food that did not upset my stomach.

As the Word and the Holy Spirit worked within me, faith began to grow. I didn't understand God and I knew I could never be good enough to approach him. Most of the time, I did not even believe in him, because I couldn't see beyond my limited senses. I only knew I could not cope with life—with my life. Only God could save me from myself and this trauma. "For it is by grace you have been saved, through faith—and this not from yourselves, it is the gift of

God" (Ephesians 2:8). Faith in God is a gift that comes from God himself.

Faith happens to people without conscious effort and without having to have all the answers. It happened that way to Christian believers in Achaia (See Acts 18:27-28). Achaia was the Roman province on the southern part of the Greek peninsula. Its capital was Corinth. The Achaians had heard the gospel about Jesus Christ, probably from the Apostle Paul. They had believed his message, but since they were new in the faith, they could not argue against verbal attacks by the synagogue rulers.

Along came a disciple named Apollos. He was a Jew, an educated man, and a gifted preacher. The passage in Acts 18 tells us that, "On arriving, he was a great help to those who by grace had believed. For he vigorously refuted the Jews in public debate, proving from the Scriptures that Jesus was the Christ." Like the Achaians, I gradually came to believe by God's grace, though I did not have much knowledge of theology to argue in support of my faith.

By the beginning of September, my ongoing letter to Ralph was reflecting the change in my thinking. I wrote: "I think I believe this Jesus may be from God, may have risen from the dead, and that his spirit may be a personal influence for good and well-being in our lives today. I believe there is some spirit or force we can't define caring for us right now and that the God represented by this spirit must have some positive plan for your physical life on earth. I believe this because I can see how far it (God or his spirit) has brought you from the shadow of death four months ago."

I listed my hopes for Ralph's recovery, and then continued my tenuous statement of faith. "And I believe that the motivator that will get us both through the years of your rehabilitation is a power much greater than ours which was demonstrated by a man named Jesus who overcame the greatest physical impairment of all—death." It was radically different from the view I quoted earlier in chapter five.

The following week, late at night, my tone was again doubting, depressed, despairing and bitter as I wrote to my husband. However, there's a significant difference; in the middle of the tirade, I cried out *to* God, not about God.

"I'm exhausted, I'm cracking. I can't search any more for the answers to all my 'whys.' I can't keep manufacturing hope. We've been asking for a fish and all God is dishing up is scorpions. I cry all the time. I'm so damn lonely, and I miss you so much. This certainly isn't life anymore. It's ugly. It's painful. It's hell. If there is a God of love and mercy, it's not in this world. Jesus didn't die to take away suffering; you've suffered every bit as much as he, and he only had to endure a few hours. *God, we've had enough!* I can't stop crying; crying for you, Ralph, about you, for our little girls who have been yanked so cruelly out of childhood, for our loss. All I believe right now is that I love you, Ralph, I need you, and I hate my life just as surely as you must hate yours."

Four and a half months had passed since Ralph's brain hemorrhage. My birthday was approaching, and I was not looking forward to it. My parents wanted to come help me celebrate. I had nothing to celebrate. The children asked what I wanted for my birthday. I said, "Nothing." I wanted to ignore the day. It could never equal the memory of the last birthday Ralph and the girls had given me.

With "help" from 5-year-old Jenny and 3-year-old Amy, Ralph had fixed his "famous" birthday dinner chili, while I used the time to work on a writing job with a fast-approaching deadline. The chili was not quite done when Ralph came up to the study carrying a box of cake mix.

"Jenny says we hafta make a cake. Can I use this?" He looked tired after a stressful day at the office, but he had insisted on doing dinner that night instead of waiting for the weekend.

"I really don't need a cake. Dinner and this time to get some work done is all I want."

Ralph sighed. "I know. I told her that, but she insists we can't have a birthday party for Mommy without a cake."

I looked at the box in his hand. "Well, you could follow the alternate directions for making a pound cake out of that. That takes only one pan and doesn't need frosting, and we could eat it warm if need be. It's getting late."

He turned the box over and read the pound cake directions. "Hmmm. That doesn't sound too bad. I was afraid I'd have to make frosting, too."

A little while later, we ate dinner with lemon pound cake baking in the oven. Afterwards, I retreated upstairs to write, while Ralph and the girls put the finishing touches on the cake. When they called me down again, I was quite impressed with their creation. They had decorated the top with powdered sugar and a few candles, and it looked GOOD.

Ralph turned out the lights, and they sang "Happy Birthday"— the girls in their off-key childish sopranos, Ralph in his off-key tenor. Then I had to blow out the candles. In the darkness, the girls squealed with delight. When Ralph turned the lights back on, we saw that I had blown all the powdered sugar off the cake. It was covering the dark, wood-grained tabletop in a nice, even dusting. Ralph and I laughed until we cried.

Mom and Dad arrived from Pittsburgh a couple of days before my birthday in September 1978. They asked how I wanted to celebrate the day. I said I wanted to spend some extra time at the hospital with Ralph. They said that was fine. They would take care of the girls and fix dinner. I was glad they were not insisting on making a big deal of it. Maybe I could get through the day despite the memories of better times.

The night before my birthday, I decided that only one gift could top powdered sugar on (or off) a pound cake and only Jesus could give it. So I prayed, "Jesus, I still have so many questions, but I choose to believe you are God's Son as the Bible says. I need your presence in my life. Please come, fill me with your Holy Spirit and help me."

Then I went to sleep. That's all. No flashes of light. No heavenly visions or voices. The next morning I awoke without stomach pains. I didn't need the Valium. I spent an ordinary day at the hospital, holding Ralph's hand, talking to him, feeding him. An unordinary peaceful calm followed me. I could not explain it except to conclude that this must be what it means to be "born again."

Chapter 9 Awakenings

My long, detailed letter to Ralph ended after October, because I no longer felt the need to pour out my soul to impersonal paper. Ralph was more alert and responding consistently, and I could talk to Jesus as well. In a short addendum dated February 12, 1979, I wrote: "In October, I began to feel confident that you were understanding and remembering things I talked to you about. So the past four months have been spent battling to get others to realize that you are a rational, thinking human being trapped inside an inoperative body."

From September 1978, until Ralph went to MossRehab Hospital in January 1979, events seemed to happen very quickly. Memories of those incidents come to me like short video clips.

The basement psychologist's office at Temple Hospital was the scene of Ralph's weekly visits with Jenny and Amy. Usually, the psychologist would leave us alone for family time. The girls would bring toys and drawing materials to show Dad. Sometimes they played with the toys the psychologist kept there including assorted artificial limbs and crutches. They did not seem intimidated by hospital paraphernalia and readily climbed the wheelchair to give Dad a kiss. They learned to ask him questions and asked him to give two blinks or a hand squeeze if his answer was "yes." They shared my joy when Ralph was able to say each of our names and "I love you." They drew pictures and listened as I read stories from the Bible about Jesus healing people.

In October, Fred was moved into the same room with Ralph. When I could not be there, Fred's mother, Nancy, kept an eye on Ralph, too, and called the nurses if he seemed uncomfortable. It was like having a real, live guardian angel present all day every day. The thought that Nancy was checking on Ralph and praying for us was comforting. I was beginning to put more stock in the results of prayer—beginning to experience the difference inside me that made Nancy so different on the outside.

Bernice phoned one evening to check on us. We had been close friends before Ralph's brain hemorrhage. She and Rod were the first ones I called for help. I had clung to them for the first two weeks. Then they gently and firmly removed themselves from my clutches. That was good. I needed to be less dependent on them. Bernice's calls were infrequent, now, but their theme was consistent: Nancy, why are you still going to the hospital every day? They're doing all they can for Ralph. You've got to think of yourself. You've got to think of your children. Her voice was always sad and shaky with emotion.

This time, when Bernice called, I tried to head off her gloom. I told her about the other Nancy, how encouraging she had been, how she was praying for our little daily needs, and how we were seeing progress. Bernice got very upset and said I was not being realistic. I assured her I was okay. I tried to tell her something about my new faith in Jesus and the peace I was experiencing. She started crying and hung up on me.

The next time I saw our friends, Bernice would not talk to me. She left the room, and Rod began asking questions about Ralph's condition, hinting at the hopelessness of his ever returning to a level of function close to his old self. "Yes," I said, "I know how bad it is. I am living with it every day. I also know I cannot live any longer with pessimism, fear, and doubt. I need hope to go on taking care of the children and myself. I have found a sustaining hope."

Whenever Tom and Jeanette came for a weekend, they brought something to help stimulate Ralph's mind. They obviously spent time between visits searching for ideas. We wondered if Ralph still had the ability to read. In large block letters, I wrote a simple command on a piece of paper: blink your eyes. When we showed it to Ralph, he blinked. I wrote, raise your right hand. He raised his right hand a little. We cheered. Tom set to work devising paper games.

We asked Ralph true/false questions, putting "true" on one edge of the paper and "false" on the opposite. We told Ralph to look at the answer he wanted. By watching his eyes, we could tell which one he was choosing. Then we tried multiple choice questions. We would point to the three or four choices one at a time and tell Ralph to blink slowly when we pointed to the right one. (A slow deliberate blink is easier to distinguish from a reflex blink.) Ralph easily passed each test. Some even brought a that's-a-dumb-question smile to his face.

While I went to check with nurses and therapists about treatments, Tom made up math problems for Ralph. When I came back, Tom showed me the results. Every response was correct, from simple arithmetic to geometry, to algebra, to . . . what-is-that-last-problem? "Oh, it's calculus," Tom said. "He got that right, too."

One day I found myself talking with a neurology resident in the hallway near the nurses' station. He was saying, "This is much harder on you than it is on Ralph, because he doesn't know how bad off he is. My grandmother had a stroke. She's just like him." I could not believe what I was hearing. I turned and walked away, thinking, "Ralph knows calculus. How can he not know how bad off he is?" Sometimes it wasn't worth arguing with doctors.

We had a peach of a social worker at Temple Hospital. I'll call her Laura. Ralph was at Temple for nine months. After three months, when it was apparent that his major medical insurance would soon be exhausted, Laura sent us to a helpful lady in the finance office who applied for Medicaid for us. After five months, Laura told us she was looking for a rehab program for him, but we might want to check out some nursing homes as alternatives. A social worker often gets the distasteful task of telling the family that the doctors can do no more for their patient. Laura did that with gentle encouragement.

The nursing homes I visited reeked of hopelessness and death. One by one I rejected them and reported my verdicts to Laura. After more than eight months, Ralph was accepted at MossRehab Hospital. (And we thought getting into college was hard!) During his last week at Temple, conversations with other staff members gave me clues that Laura had fought very hard, possibly jeopardizing her job, to keep Ralph from a death-row sentence to a nursing home.

Our families were as supportive, sympathetic, and encouraging as possible from a distance. They called at least once a week. Dad had recently retired, so he and Mom came often to help for a few days during the week. The Unks clan came for weekend visits: Ed and Kay with their daughters Sue and Debbie, Ralph's younger brother Bruce and his wife Patty, and Mom Unks. Sometimes Mom Unks would stay longer, and I would put her on a bus for the return trip the following week.

During these family visits, the relatives took over cooking and babysitting. Jenny and Amy had time with their grandparents, aunts, and cousins. I spent more time with Ralph, and Ralph seemed more responsive when his brothers livened up the visit. Before Ralph's illness, planning for houseguests used to get me nervous and upset. I would spend days planning the food and cleaning the house, being crabby and irritable. After he was stricken, I welcomed company, gave them sheets to make their own beds, and directed them to the nearest supermarket. Cleaning? Who would notice dirt with so many feet tracking in more? I didn't even mind when one group arrived only two hours after the last one left.

I shared my questions about God with my family. I wanted their conservative, main-line protestant opinions about what I was hearing concerning healing and the Holy Spirit. Mom went with me to Bible study. She said she was glad I had found such a supportive group. One Saturday night in November, Dad accompanied me to a healing service. I had never been to one, so I went with fearful curiosity. There we heard people praising in the Spirit with unintelligible tongues, a musically harmonious chorus of voices swelling in crescendo to God. There was nothing scary about it. In fact, the sound was quite heavenly. Dad did not seem to think we heard anything unusual. He said it was a very nice service.

Mom Unks accompanied me to Bible study one week. As the women prayed for Ralph and for her, she was moved to tears. I began to glimpse her mother's grief over what had happened to her son. Later, she went with me to the hospital and spent over an hour talking with the psychologist by herself. For the rest of the week, Mom went on a window washing campaign. Ralph's response to emotional stress had also been to immerse himself in physical labor. Mom and I had opportunities to talk after the girls were in bed. She, too, was struggling with doubts about God and his love and care, as she watched her son suffering.

Over several months, some of the women in the Bible study began to be more open about using what they referred to as their prayer language. During those times, the atmosphere of love and peace in the room seemed especially comforting. When I had told Jesus that I chose to believe in him, I had asked for his Holy Spirit to fill me and help me. Was that the same as asking for the baptism of the Holy Spirit, I wondered? Could I also pray in tongues? Peg told me, "The Holy Spirit is a gentleman. He will never force anyone to do anything they don't want to do. Praying what sounds like nonsense words may feel silly at first, but you are speaking to God as Paul says in 1 Corinthians 14:2. God understands you"

I decided to try it. Soon I discovered that I could sing in the Spirit while driving to the hospital when I was alone in the car. Singing praises with the Spirit of the Lord calmed my apprehensions about what I might find when I got there and gave me strength to deal with the day.

Chapter 10 A Rolling Chair Gathers No Moss

On a snowy day near the end of January 1979, I rode with Ralph in an ambulance from Temple Hospital twenty blocks up Broad Street to Einstein Medical Center and MossRehab Hospital. Despite the dreary weather and treacherous travel, it was a happy event. In the first two days at Moss, our whirlwind orientation promised change and bolstered hope. I was instructed to bring clothes for Ralph—no more hospital gowns. The next day he was dressed and placed in a reclining wheelchair. Therapy sessions filled most of his day and his meals were fed to him in the dining room. Except for weekly meetings with therapists, my visiting was restricted to evenings and weekends.

During those visits, I read to him from a book that had been given to me by one of the Bible study ladies. It was *Caught Up Into Paradise* by Richard E. Eby, D.O.[1] The physician author of the book had suffered a severe brain injury in a fall. In fact he died and experienced what he describes as the anteroom of heaven. Urgent prayers by many friends helped bring him back to life. Several years later, after full recovery and rehabilitation, Dr. Eby experienced a vision of hell while touring the tomb of Lazarus on a trip to the Holy Land. In his book, he describes not only his injury, but both heaven and hell with a scientist's eye for detail.

My reason for reading the book to Ralph was to encourage him. This was a case of healing from a severe brain injury. It was well documented and published by a major book company. Equally compelling were Dr. Eby's descriptions of the heaven to be gained and the hell avoided by faith in Jesus Christ. Ralph listened as I read. He seemed alert and attentive but showed no reaction until I got to the description of hell. Then he began moaning. Thinking he was moaning because he was uncomfortable, I stopped to reposition him. When I resumed reading, he resumed moaning.

The hell Dr. Eby describes is one of total separation from everyone and everything. Terrifying isolation from which he could not break free. Nothing to see. Nothing to do. Bone chilling cold. Horrid smell. Nausea. Taunting demons damning God. Intense emotions of fear, anger, loneliness. Total despair of ever escaping.

---

[1] Richard E. Eby, D.O., *Caught Up Into Paradise*, Old Tappan, NJ: Fleming H. Revell, Co., (1978)

Attempting to scream, but unable to make a sound. A sense of impending insanity.[2]

Ralph's moaning intensified as I read. I asked him; "Does this sound like what you have been going through?" He said, "Uh huh." Of course! He had been living in hell for the past ten months. I read over some of the individual points in the description again, questioning Ralph's experience of each one. For each, he affirmed, "Uh huh." Finally, I asked, "Do you mean you have even heard demons taunting?" Once again, "Uh huh."

This was the first indication I had that Ralph, too, was struggling with spiritual questions. The book helped him give verbal description to his silent suffering. With his adamant "Uh huhs," he affirmed the existence of a sinister spiritual world. Surely, I thought, the Holy Spirit must be just as real. Only the Spirit's presence could counteract those taunting demons. I resolved to seek ways to bring the Spirit of Christ into Ralph's experience, at least in our times together.

Ralph's doctor gave permission for the girls to visit on weekends, and we looked forward all week to Sunday afternoon family time. It represented progress toward the goal of being together again at home. However, my goal and the hospital's were not exactly the same. Mine was to get Ralph well before he

---

[2] Eby, *Caught Up Into Paradise*, 229-230.

came home. Theirs was to get him out of there. After two months, the social worker—who was not nearly as supportive as Laura at Temple had been—called me to her office to talk about Ralph's discharge. If I had not been sitting already, I am sure my knees would have buckled from the shock.

"But he's not ready to come home," I said. "What about all the things they were going to teach him to do here? And the special equipment they were going to build for him?"

"He's not making progress fast enough to justify his staying here."

"He can't come home, yet. We have a two-story house, and the bedrooms are all upstairs."

The social worker showed no compassion. "Occupational therapy and the nursing staff will be working with you to teach you how to manage his care. They may be able to send a team out to your home to recommend adaptations."

"How long before . . .?"

"Our goal is to discharge him by the first of May. Now about making arrangements to pay your bill . . ."

My feelings went numb as my brain switched to automatic mode. I have foggy, nightmarish recollections of sitting across a desk from a hospital employee and signing stacks of forms. Social security disability payments had begun, but Medicare would not take effect until two years later, so we would have to buy, rent, borrow, or improvise all the equipment Ralph would need. *We?* Ralph could do nothing. The kids were too young and relatives were too far away. Make that *I*. I had to do it all.

I attended Ralph's therapy sessions during the day. I fed him and practiced caring for him on my evening visits. I made trips to the county offices in Norristown to apply for medical assistance to help pay his hospital bill. I searched bulletin boards and classified ads for used hospital equipment for sale. Remember the young doctor whose grandmother had had a stroke? I bought a hospital bed from him after she died. I wondered if she gave up because her grandson assumed she was a vegetable and did not try to communicate with her.

Friends helped get a space ready for Ralph at home. We took apart the dining room table and stored it in the basement. The hospital bed took its place in the dining room. I made a muslin curtain for the doorway to the living room and a plastic cover for the buffet, which would serve as a dresser and wash stand. The contents of the buffet moved to other storage places and Ralph's clothes and medical supplies replaced them.

The decision to bring Ralph home was not a hard one to make. I had already visited nursing homes and rated them from undesirable to appalling. I knew home care would be work, but while I was caring for Ralph, I could also be doing laundry and have dinner in the oven. I would be home for the girls when they got home from school. Besides, there was no other option financially. A nursing home would take all of Ralph's Social Security Disability pay. The allowance for dependents would not be enough to support the girls and me and maintain the house. I would have to work full-time, arrange after school care for the girls, and spend evenings and weekends visiting Ralph and doing housework. The girls would be missing both a father and a mother.

I looked forward to Ralph's coming home so we could be together again and have emotional and perhaps some physical intimacy. I was sure I could do more therapy than they were doing in the hospital. I knew Ralph would be motivated to try harder in the more positive environment at home. He could watch the girls play, hear good music, see green grass, trees, and flowers, and familiar treasured things. Friends could come to visit more easily, he could be part of holidays, and I could fix his favorite foods. Most of all, I hoped and expected that a miracle would happen at home where we could read the Bible, listen to praise music, and pray often.

Our families and most of our friends were supportive of the decision. Some were not. Bernice and Rod tried to talk me out of it. They were convinced that I would do irreparable psychological harm to my children by having their severely disabled father in the house. They even gave me journal articles that supported their contention. When they could not dissuade me, they appealed to my parents and a few friends to try to talk sense into me. I thank God that the supportive people shielded me from further attacks.

Many months later, it occurred to me that, had I put Ralph in a nursing home, it would have given the wrong message to my children. Sending their father away could have them fearing, "What if I get sick? Will Mommy send me away, too?" I would rather have them see that families stick together and take care of each other.

Of course, one small family cannot do it alone. Again, I thank God that the supportive friends talked to their friends who talked to others, and probably all of them prayed for us. Before I knew it, a lady I had never met, who went to another church, was recruiting helpers. She wrote letters to every church within five miles and followed up with phone calls and personal visits. Her efforts netted about thirty volunteers to help with daily physical therapy for Ralph and several more to do housecleaning and yard work.

The pieces were falling into place for Ralph's homecoming— for *our* homecoming. When first confronted by the MossRehab social worker, I could echo King David's cry, "O Lord, how many are my foes! How many rise up against me!" (Psalm 3:1). By the time the anticipated day arrived, I was singing with the writer of

Lamentations. "Because of the Lord's great love, we are not consumed, for his compassions never fail. They are new every morning; great is your faithfulness" (Lamentations 3:22-23). In the social worker's office, I had felt that *I* had to do it all. A few weeks later *we* had done it—the Lord and I and all the helpers he miraculously provided.

Surgery to repair the huge decubitus ulcer on Ralph's right hip bought us an extra two weeks to prepare. On a warm day in the middle of May, Jim Bell drove me to Moss. I rode home in the transport ambulance with Ralph. Jim followed. The ambulance crew carried Ralph into the house and transferred him to his wheelchair before they left. Jim moved the refrigerator so we could get the wheelchair into the kitchen. Then he left. The visiting nurse made a brief visit and left. I was alone in the house with my husband. He was a helpless invalid. I had just become his caregiver. He could do nothing. I cried.

Chapter 11 Lonely Intimacy

When Ralph came home from rehab, I looked for ways we could enjoy a little intimacy. I tried lying next to him in bed. On his narrow hospital bed, that was not only uncomfortable but dangerous. Maybe we could cuddle on the couch. I put a stack of favorite records on the stereo and dimmed the lights. Then I proceeded to do a pivot transfer to get Ralph out of his wheelchair. Dropping him into the couch, which was lower than his chair, I fell on top of him. As I rearranged limbs and propped him with pillows, I wondered aloud, "How am I going to get you out of here again?"

The couch was not as comfortable for Ralph as his wheelchair. When he was uncomfortable, his muscles would go rigid and cramp. Pain aggravated a cycle of spasms and rigidity and more pain. It was not fun for him or for me. In fact, snuggling a department store mannequin would be less torturous. I soon began to figure out how to get him back into his wheelchair.

After half an hour of several futile attempts, I knew I could not lift him by myself. It was late in the evening. There was no one to call for help. I pushed the wheelchair away, wrestled him to the floor, rolled him from side to side to put the canvas sling for the lift under him, and used that machine to get him up from the floor. Then I pushed the lift, with Ralph dangling from it, across the living room to his bed in the dining room. Scratch romantic evenings.

Perhaps manual stimulation would give Ralph some sexual release and me a little vicarious pleasure. I tried it. For Ralph, any kind of stimulation increased his spasticity. His rigid legs would cramp painfully. Pain has a way of killing pleasure.

I threw my passion into therapy. Ralph was already receiving passive physical therapy each morning and evening from teams of volunteers. They would transfer him to the floor using the lift, then stretch, bend, and roll him, guiding his limbs through the range of motion they should normally have. I decided to spend afternoons on occupational therapy.

With his arm supported in a sling device attached to the wheelchair, Ralph could hold a spoon with a thick padded handle. He could slowly move the spoon from a dish to his mouth when I told him to. I figured all he needed to do was practice, practice, practice, and he would soon be feeding himself. How wrong I was.

While Ralph could move many muscles in response to verbal commands, he could not initiate or continue movements on his own. That was one of the subtle effects of his brain injury. It took me a long time to learn that. Meanwhile, I coached, cajoled, pleaded, commanded, begged, and nagged. As we worked, my voice became agitated, my pitch and volume higher. The harder I tried to get him to move that spoon, the less he moved it. I accused him of not trying, of not caring. Sessions ended with me walking away in tears and Ralph closing his eyes and dozing off.

Actually, the harder Ralph tried to do anything, the tenser he got, until his muscles froze and he couldn't move at all. His lack of movement was not an indication that he wasn't trying but evidence that he was trying too hard. I was frustrated by those intensive therapy sessions. He was frustrated. We set the pattern then for how we both continued to deal with frustration. I walked away and did something else. He closed his eyes and went to sleep. He would rather have walked. And I could have used a nap.

Finally, I stopped pushing therapy. We got a long-playing cassette tape player from the Association for the Blind and talking books from the Library for the Blind and Physically Handicapped. In the afternoons, I put a book on for Ralph to listen to and went upstairs to sew. Our rapport was better after that.

We could not do the things we used to do together anymore, but I still hoped for some meaningful communication. Ralph came home from rehab with an electronic box to help with that. It was about sixteen inches square with rows and columns of tiny lights. Under each light, a label designated a letter of the alphabet or a short common response such as 'yes' or 'no'. The squeeze of a switch tucked into Ralph's clenched hand would start the lights in sequence across the rows. Another squeeze would stop the lights at the letter or phrase he wanted to select. If he missed the letter he wanted, he had to wait for the lights to cycle through the whole board again. With this alphabet scanner, Ralph could spell out a three- or four-word sentence in about half an hour. If I wrote down each letter as he selected it, I could still remember the first word by the time he got to the last one. So much for conversation!

With patience and long-suffering (What else could he do?), Ralph did manage to relate some of his feelings to me. Mostly, he had to wait for me to discover them by observation and ask questions he could answer with a 'yes' or 'no' to confirm them. I found out that the one thing he most wanted to be able to do was talk. He would also have liked to make love, and he remembered when we did. When he first came home, he may have been confused about where he was, because long-term memory of his youth was better than his recall of recent places and events. His short-term memory improved with time. He did not feel internal pain such as stomach cramps. That kind of pain increased his spastic rigidity, and he felt the resulting cramps in his legs. In the middle of the night, he prayed for relief from the pain.

A search for a better communication device spanned years. Eventually, we found one, or rather, it found us. The story of Ralph's Eyegaze Communication System is a blessing I will tell you about later. Ralph needed help to use it, though. Someone else had to position him in front of the computer and be available to assist him. Someone else had to initiate relationship. It was usually up to me to do that.

Since Ralph was unable to talk, I began to discuss problems with friends instead. That was the beginning of our drifting apart. The husband who was once my best friend became a chore to be done like a house to be cleaned. My caregiving grew mechanical and one-sided. I noticed that Ralph did not look at me as intently as he used to while I bathed him. When I did try to share family concerns and household problems with him, he seemed lethargic and disinterested. On the surface, our relationship looked fine. I gave care; he received it. No fights, no arguments. In some ways, it was no better than one with open conflict. We were two strangers living together. I was too busy doing all the work to realize I was lonely. Ralph, locked inside his non-functioning body must have been excruciatingly so.

Empathy and compassion for Ralph came slowly as I learned to acknowledge my own feelings and attitudes. If I felt unloved and unlovable, he must have felt more so. If I felt rejected by God, how much more did he? If I felt isolated and trapped in my role as a caregiver, how much more intensely must he have felt his imprisonment? If I felt lonely and misunderstood, so must he. If my attitude toward his disabilities showed anger or resentment, how could his be any more accepting? If I could walk away from pain and frustration, I had to ask myself, "Who's really suffering here?"

I began to pray for insight into Ralph's feelings. I didn't want to be the nagging therapist. I needed to be a compassionate friend, advocate, and wife. How would I treat him if he were not disabled? I remembered the times during the day when I would have said "I love you," given him a kiss, or touched him in passing, and began doing those things again. I apologized for accidental bumps or spills. I added "please" and "thank you" to my requests for him to open his mouth or move a hand. Since he needed constant care like an infant, it took effort to respect him as an adult.

Ralph couldn't do anything intentional to irritate or annoy, but sometimes his involuntary spasms and moaning had that effect. I often found myself scolding or yelling in anger and frustration. This must have added to his frustration. At those times, I needed

Jesus to love him through me, with tenderness. At the same time, I needed to be tough to keep on doing the job at hand. I couldn't break down in tears and run away just because I was overwhelmed. The hardest thing I had to do was care for him when he was rigid and moaning with pain, and I could neither figure out the cause nor relieve it.

Changing my attitude and actions toward Ralph and his care was a process that took years. Some good friends helped me see that there is practical advice in Scripture. Jesus' actions and Paul's guidelines for Christian living compelled me to take an honest look at my attitudes as I performed attendant duties for Ralph. As I changed some of my actions, I noticed my attitude changing as well. And as my disposition changed, I noticed Ralph becoming more attentive and responsive. In the process, I discovered how powerless I am to change without the Holy Spirit. He transforms me with constant gentle tending.

Chapter 12 A Bruised Reed Gently Tended

People often urged me, "Do something for yourself." It was well-intended advice, usually meaning I should indulge in some decadent luxury for respite from the demands of caregiving. To me, decadent luxury would simply have been eight hours of uninterrupted sleep.

In the early 1980's, a husband and wife, whom we had met through one of the Bible study ladies, offered to stay with Ralph and the girls for a weekend so I could go on a retreat. They came twice beforehand to get acquainted. I showed them how to do Ralph's personal care—change the catheter, dress him, transfer him, feed him, give him drinks—and how to position him in bed at night. I prepared food for the weekend and wrote instructions. By the time I left for the retreat, I was exhausted from preparation.

My first night away in a strange place was not very restful. The next morning, I was summoned out of the first session for a phone call. Heart pounding and fearing the worst, I heard our substitute caregivers say that something was wrong with Ralph. He was unconscious. They couldn't wake him to eat.

"Did he sleep during the night?" I asked.

"Oh, yes. He slept all night."

"When you checked on him in the night, what did he look like?"

"His eyes were closed."

"But was he relaxed? Were his arms limp and head drooping?"

"I didn't touch him, didn't want to disturb him."

"Was he breathing deeply or snoring?"

"Yes, he was breathing real heavy."

"Like panting? Were the bed clothes wet with sweat when you gave him his bath?"

"Well, yea, I guess they were kind of sweaty."

"Then he was not comfortable during the night. He probably did not sleep at all, so he's exhausted now. Recline his wheelchair and let him sleep a couple hours. Then try to wake him up again and get some drinks into him."

If I had driven to the retreat, I would have left then. However, I had come with three other women, and I was captive. I called home three times, worried a lot, and didn't sleep much better the second night. The only thing I got out of the retreat was a Bible verse that one of the leaders gave me as a personal prophecy when she prayed for me. "Delight yourself in the Lord and he will give you the desires of your heart" (Psalm 37:4). The one desire of my heart was healing for my husband. I would certainly try my best to delight in the Lord if he would fulfill that promise. (Doesn't that sound like I was still trying to bargain with God?) As soon as I got home, our substitute caregivers bolted. It took me several days to repair the damage from the weekend and catch up on lost sleep.

Obviously, vacations provided no respite. Many people asked, "Isn't there a support group you can go to?" How could I go to meetings when I barely had time to take a shower? Besides, morose fellow caregivers were the last people I wanted to hang out with. The "normal" people who loaned a little time and a listening ear became my support group. Many of them were volunteers who came to help with Ralph's exercise. They showed us God's love with simple acts and casual conversation.

Marty became my mentor, peer-counselor, and close friend. Since I could not go to Bible study on Tuesday mornings, she would come another afternoon to visit. When I lamented that I had no time to make a favorite desert for Ralph, she brought a cheesecake the next week. Sometimes she would read to Ralph while I went out to do errands. She helped most by sharing her own problems, fears, and faith, including her questions and doubts. As she revealed how the Holy Spirit helped her solve problems through Scripture passages, she helped me learn how God could guide me.

The first time I experienced God speaking to me through his Word, it concerned fear. Fear had been my constant companion since the day of Ralph's brain hemorrhage, taking only a brief holiday when I first asked Jesus to be part of my life. Fear made its physical presence felt in the pit of my stomach by day. It haunted my dreams at night. I thought, "Okay, if we get through this, if Ralph recovers and regains function, do we live in dread of another brain hemorrhage? After all, the surgeon never found the source of the bleed. And what if something happens to me? Or to one of the girls?" I could not stand another catastrophe. That would crush my shaky new faith.

One night when the fears and what-ifs were especially strong, I sought solace in the Bible. I remembered that Marty had told me about a passage that helped her when she was a new Christian. It is in Isaiah, written nearly 700 years before Jesus' time, but it is a prophecy from God about Jesus, the Messiah.

"Here is my servant, whom I uphold, my chosen one in whom I delight; I will put my Spirit on him and he will bring justice to the nations. He will not shout or cry out, or raise his voice in the streets. A bruised reed he will not break, and a smoldering wick he will not snuff out" (Isaiah 42:1-3a).

I was a bruised reed in need of gentle tending and support. I was a smoldering candlewick just beginning to burn and in need of protection from gusts. I read on. The chapter tells of wonderful things the Messiah will do—open blind eyes and free captives. It contains words of praise for the Lord who will not forsake his people. It gives warnings to those who trust in idols. Then, the beginning of chapter 43 caught my eye.

"But now, this is what the Lord says—he who created you, O Jacob, he who formed you, O Israel: 'Fear not for I have redeemed you; I have summoned you by name; you are mine. When you pass through the waters, I will be with you; and when you pass through the rivers, they will not sweep over you. When you walk through the fire, you will not be burned; the flames will not set you ablaze. For I am the Lord, your God, the Holy One of Israel, your Savior; . . . Since you are precious and honored in my sight, and because I love you . . . **Do not be afraid, for I am with you'"** (Isaiah 43:1-5, emphasis added).

Tears began to fill my eyes as I continued to read. Through the rest of chapters 43 and 44, words of encouragement seemed to jump off the page in boldface letters.

"Forget the former things; **do not dwell on the past**. I am making a way in the desert and streams in the wasteland" (43:18, 19b).

"This is what the Lord says—he who made you, who formed you in the womb, and who will help you: **Do not be afraid** . . ." (44:2).

"I will pour out my Spirit on your offspring, and my **blessing on your descendants**" (44:3).

"**Do not tremble, do not be afraid**" (44:8).

I heard God speaking reassurance to me through those words. By the time I finished chapter 44, I was crying so hard I could no longer read, but the fear was gone. The possibility that Ralph might suffer another brain hemorrhage still existed, but my fear of it did not. In fact, when the Lord takes him home, I thought, a quick, massive bleed may be one of the more merciful ways he could do it.

After that night with Isaiah, the peace I felt when I first asked Jesus to be part of my life returned, pushing out the fear. I had described the feeling in the long letter that I wrote to Ralph in the hospital. "It was nothing dramatic, nothing anybody else could see. I just felt good all day—calm, peaceful, full of faith and hope. I even felt very patient and tolerant with the kids that evening."

My next paragraph, written less than three weeks later revealed a relapse in my state of mind. "The next day I had a few fights with the kids and was a bit more irritable again. We've had good times and bad times like that ever since. However, underlying it all there seems to be a basic faith and hopefulness that I didn't have before. It's there even when I mess up and yell at the kids or express some of the old doubts. I don't think the Spirit of Jesus came and left again; it's just that I haven't learned how to let it live and work in me all the time, yet. The old crabby, cynical me still comes through at times, even though the new faith and love from the Holy Spirit are there, too. I guess maybe that's what free will is. We constantly have the option to choose between the worldly part of us and letting the Spirit work through us."

The battle went on. In my heart, there was tension between "the peace of God, which transcends all understanding" (Philippians 4:7) and its antithesis—confusion, turmoil, conflict, and chaos. When peace slipped away from me, paralyzing emotions crept in—fear, frustration, anger, hate, resentment, self-pity, and guilt. These sapped the energy my caregiving duties demanded. Fatigue and depression resulted. It was easier to feel peaceful when my surroundings were tranquil, but the constant demands of my daily life were often anything but. In those early years of faith, I needed help to hear from the Holy Spirit and resolve the negative emotions. That's where my "Tuesday Group" came in.

Chapter 13 Tuesday Issues

The Tuesday group started when Marty asked if I would like to join her and a mutual friend, Jane, to do some simple Christmas handcrafts. While stitching felt tree ornaments, we talked about our families, foibles, fears, and faith. The problems we encountered between our times together were similar, so we would get out a Bible to look up a passage we thought might be relevant. Soon we were each bringing Bibles and notebooks, sharing more and stitching less. After Christmas, we kept on meeting.

By then, a home health aide made it possible for me to go out twice a week, so for the next six years, Marty, Jane and I were together almost every Tuesday morning. Always, the problems we shared had similar themes. Often, we found that we had gone to the same Scripture verses for help. When the passages were not the same, they complimented each other. Unmistakably, the Holy Spirit was leading. We helped each other think more about Jesus and imitate his love. We let the Word speak to us without trying to add worldly advice, and we prayed together.

The group grew to include six to ten women at various times. Most of us had motherhood in common, though our children ranged in age from toddlers to adults. None of the others were long-term caregivers, but we experienced the same emotional struggles. Fear, guilt, anger, self-pity, envy, resentment, rejection, and discouragement were some of our Tuesday issues. No matter what circumstances cause those problems, God's solutions are the same. As we prayed the problems to God, his answers came to us.

We would start by thanking God for our time together, with each person adding short one- or two-sentence prayers as she felt led. We went on to words of praise and then our concerns. When one person mentioned a personal problem, others would pray for her and for the Spirit's work in her heart and the situation. We kept Bibles open during prayer time. Often, one person would read a relevant verse of scripture. God's word became part of the prayer and the answer. Between concerns, we thanked God and spent long moments in silence enjoying his presence. Heartfelt songs of praise and love for Jesus concluded those times after 15, 20, 30 minutes or more.

Sometimes we felt the presence of the Holy Spirit in tangible ways: tears, warmth, or a sensation of oneness with each other and the Lord, where walls, furnishings, and distractions seemed to fade away. I am confident the Spirit was present, even when sensations were not. Jesus tells us so. "For where two or three come together in my name, there am I with them" (Matthew 18:20).

For me, the power of God's Spirit was most noticeable in what I was able to accomplish the rest of the day. Tuesday mornings I sometimes awakened thinking I had too much to do and no time for the group. However, I came home from our meetings with renewed energy and a clear mind to work more efficiently. I was usually able to accomplish more than I had planned, and I did it with joy while humming a praise chorus. That's when I perceived practical ways to translate the peace I felt with God into a more peaceful home by reducing noise, clutter, confusion, and conflict.

Searching the Bible for God's encouragement on Tuesday mornings led us repeatedly to Paul's letter to the church at Philippi. "Rejoice in the Lord always. I will say it again: Rejoice! Let your gentleness be evident to all. The Lord is near. Do not be anxious about anything, but in everything, by prayer and petition, with thanksgiving, present your requests to God. And the peace of God, which transcends all understanding will guard your hearts and your minds in Christ Jesus" (Philippians 4:4-7).

Rejoice in the Lord. Do not be anxious. Do not be afraid. Pray. Those are commands from God, not suggestions. Rejoice in the midst of strife when you think you have nothing to rejoice about. For our obedience, God promises that his peace will guard our hearts and minds. Rejoicing also results in gentleness of spirit.

There is a less obvious command in that passage: let the gentleness that results from rejoicing be evident to all. It is easy to appear gentle in public. It's hard to be gentle all the time with those closest to us. I have already confessed to yelling at Ralph. I allowed his painful spasticity and involuntary moaning to frustrate me, and yelled at him for something he couldn't control. On more than one occasion, I accidentally hurt him by handling him too roughly when he was especially rigid. Enter guilt, another of those crippling negative emotions.

Philippians 4:5 brings two separate thoughts together: "Let your gentleness be evident to all. The Lord is near." For a long time, guilt over my lack of gentleness made me view the nearness of the Lord as a threat. I felt that he was watching my every ungentle move to criticize and condemn. Now, I think the statement "The Lord is near" belongs better with the next sentence in verse 6. The Lord is near so we can talk to him anytime; therefore, we should not be anxious, even when we lose our gentleness and self-control. Take the matter to God in prayer and his peace will return.

"In everything, by prayer and petition, *with thanksgiving*, present your requests to God" (v. 6). On Tuesdays, we were learning to thank God for his answers even before we knew them. We were also learning that prayer is more than petitions (requests). It is open, honest communication. It is telling God how we feel about our problems. Telling him our frustrations and worries. Telling God when we are angry with him and confessing when we take that anger out on people.

Prayer is also receiving assurance from God that he hears and understands—Holy Spirit comfort. It comes from knowing that God forgives our sins because Jesus paid the penalty for them on the cross. Jesus' sacrifice is the only thing that enables us to be at peace with God; that is, to have the right to come to him in prayer without fear of condemnation. We get peace by believing Jesus. I felt it the day I believed. Two more verses from Philippians contain down-to-earth advice for maintaining peace.

"Finally brothers, whatever is true, whatever is noble, whatever is right, whatever is pure, whatever is admirable—if anything is excellent or praiseworthy—think about such things. Whatever you have learned or received or heard from me, or seen in me—put it into practice. And the God of peace will be with you" (Philippians 4:8-9).

What or who is truly true, noble, right, pure, admirable and praiseworthy? Only Jesus, of course. What do we learn or receive from the Apostle Paul in his letters? The good news about Jesus. What do we see in Paul? A life dedicated to Jesus and continually becoming more Christ-like. On Tuesday mornings, we helped each other to do that.

Another big Tuesday issue was guilt. I've mentioned my feelings of guilt over hurting Ralph or getting angry with him for being so tense, even though I knew his rigid muscles resulted from his brain injury, and he could not control them. I failed him in other ways, also. I would get busy with my work and neglect to give him a drink as often as I should. I failed to wake up to reposition him in the night. I parked him in front of the TV instead of taking time to communicate with him. I didn't take him out as much as I could, because I was too tired. Sure, I had plausible excuses for all my failures as a caregiver, but I still felt guilty.

The guilt went deeper than my failures. It reached into the past and caused me to question God. Did my propensity for worry and fear cause this tragedy in the first place? Could I have prevented it? Ralph had a killer headache just about two weeks before the massive hemorrhage; maybe if I had insisted he see a doctor then . . . Had my lack of sufficient faith prevented Ralph from receiving a healing? Had my selfish prayers for his healing kept God from taking him home where he could be free? I knew that the answer to all of these questions is an emphatic NO.

I still felt guilty. In fact, I was guilty—guilty of fear and worry, but that did not cause Ralph's brain to bleed. Prevention would have required medical knowledge and foresight neither Ralph nor

I had at the time, so I was guilty of applying hindsight and regret to the situation. Worst of all, I was guilty of being terribly egotistical to think that my prayers and the strength of my faith controlled God's actions toward Ralph.

There is only one solution to my guilt. It is the Gospel of Jesus Christ. God's Word explains it. First, the Word shows me that I am not alone in my sin.

"There is not a righteous man on earth who does what is right and never sins" (Ecclesiastes 7:20).

However, God does not reject me because of my shortcomings. Nor does he reject anyone else.

"For God so loved the world that he gave his one and only Son, that whoever believes in him shall not perish but have eternal life" (John 3:16).

Christ took the ultimate punishment for all of my sins when he willingly allowed himself to be executed by being nailed to a cross like the worst criminals of his day. His sacrifice takes away my sinfulness. All I have to do is believe.

"Therefore, there is now no condemnation for those who are in Christ Jesus" (Romans 8:1).

When I came to Jesus, I came as a victim, desperately seeking help to deal with a tragedy beyond my control. I did not have a sense of guilt. I did not repent of any wrongdoing, since I had done nothing to deserve punishment that I could see. The better I get to know Jesus, the more I see how sinful I really am. Every day I reject God, try to manage things on my own, and fail to trust him. When I first began to be aware of my sins, I doubted my salvation. Yet, God had rewarded my decision to believe in Jesus by freeing me from the Valium and giving me his Holy Spirit and his peace. Another quote from John is enlightening.

"Whoever believes in him is not condemned, but whoever does not believe stands condemned already because he has not believed in the name of God's one and only Son" (John 3:18).

My choosing to believe in Jesus was actually repentance. By making that decision, I turned away from the sin of my previous unbelief. Despite the fact that I did not know disbelief was a sin, I received salvation at the time. From that point on, I was no longer condemned for my sins, known or unknown. From that point on, nothing could separate me from the love of God that is in Christ Jesus (See Romans 8:39).

That is, nothing outside of me can separate me from God's love. I often separate myself from his love. That's what happens when I submit to guilty feelings though I know Jesus has removed the actual guilt. That's what is happening when I allow anger, self-pity, and discouragement to rob me of the peace, joy, and hope that I have through Jesus. That's why I need regular encouragement from other Christians who direct me to Scripture's remedies for my crippling negative emotions.

One of the worst of the negatives is anger. In our Tuesday conversations, Jane and I discovered that we both had a problem with it. I'm not talking about justifiable indignation over a specific assault, leading one to confront and resolve the problem. I mean generalized wrath simmering under the surface, frequently erupting in grumpiness, tears, or violence toward inanimate objects. Such passion almost never solves anything and can hurt the angry one or someone else.

For me, the problem went back to long before Ralph's brain hemorrhage. Our basement door still bears the scar from a time when I kicked it in fury over who-knows-what. Another time, I stormed out of the house and got in the car. Ralph followed me, took my keys from the ignition, and walked back in the house without saying a word. When I calmed down and went inside, he handed me the keys and said, "I didn't think it was safe for you to drive." I put the keys back in my purse and took off my coat.

The stress of my caregiving role brought latent anger to the surface. My rough handling of Ralph came from anger, which grew out of frustration. Not only did I hurt him, but I hurt myself. When I was lifting or turning Ralph, I was most likely to strain muscles when angry. Thank God for a friend with whom I could share the problem. Together, Jane and I found godly and constructive ways to deal with anger.

God is not against anger. He is against sin. In the Old Testament, we read about many times when he became angry with his wayward children. We also read that he "is slow to anger and abounding in love." Anger is an emotion. It is not a sin. God created us with the ability to feel. What we do with the anger we feel can become sinful.

Jesus became angry only rarely. Not when he threw the moneychangers out of the temple. Not when Satan tempted him in the desert. Not when he cursed the fig tree. The Bible doesn't use the word anger or any of its synonyms to describe Jesus at those times. Jesus was indignant when his disciples kept the children away. He called the little ones over and blessed them (See Mark 10:14). He became angry when he met a man with a withered hand in the synagogue—angry at the self-righteous worshipers who refused to take a stand for helping this poor man on the Sabbath. (See Mark 3:1-5). What Jesus did with his anger was to heal the man with the shriveled hand. Jesus is our model for dealing with anger.

I had to learn that the first thing to do when I feel angry is nothing. I ask, what is the real source of my anger? Could it be my own frustration and fatigue? Am I angry with any person, myself included, or am I angry with God for allowing this situation? Many times, I discover that behind the flare-ups is my own ongoing struggle with the question of why evil exists. In other words, I am angry with God. It's okay to tell that to God. When I am honest with him about my feelings, then he can help and comfort me.

Some ways the Spirit showed us to deal with anger include writing down feelings, praying about them and then tearing them up. Singing or listening to praise music helps. Working at some constructive physical activity turns anger energy into positive energy. I can also try to avoid situations I know will set me off. Finally, I need to work at adopting positive virtues that counteract anger. "Therefore, as God's chosen people, holy and dearly loved, clothe yourselves with compassion, kindness, humility, gentleness and patience" (Colossians 3:12).

If I am totally honest with myself, I must admit that some of my anger stems from self-pity. What does God's word have to say about self-pity? When offered the opportunity to feel sorry for himself, Jesus rejected the idea. He had just finished telling his disciples that he would suffer at the hands of the religious leaders, that he would be killed, and would be raised to life on the third day. Peter did not like what he heard, especially the words 'suffer' and 'killed.' Apparently, he missed the part about resurrection. He took Jesus aside and told him, 'No way! Never!' "Jesus turned and said to Peter, 'Get behind me Satan! You are a stumbling block to me; you do not have in mind the things of God, but the things of men'" (Matthew 16:23).

Practically speaking, self-pity is my "stumbling block". It does not solve my problems. It saps energy. It leads to envy, resentment, and anger. Anger makes me do things I regret, which leads to guilt. Guilt destroys my peace with my heavenly Father and my ability to cope with daily demands. I feel frustrated, weak, tired, and discouraged. Poor me. Poor, poor me. The only thing that will stop the negative cycle is to stop pitying myself. Shed the tears, yes, but shed them while crying out to God. Let him give me his mercy. Renew my commitment to trust him with details. Ask his forgiveness for allowing my negative emotions to rule. Then, turn off the tears and get back to work.

God has already provided the antidote for all our negatives. It is Jesus. In him we are totally accepted and unconditionally loved. We have hope for the future, which gives us peace and joy in the present. The joy of the Lord is our strength (See Nehemiah 8:10). Moreover, our present sufferings are not worth comparing with the glory we will see when we are resurrected with Jesus (See Romans 8:18-25).

On Tuesday mornings, Jane used to greet everyone in the group with a hug, a smile, and the words, "Peace and joy!" Whenever her week had been especially trying, she hugged harder, smiled more broadly, and put more enthusiasm than usual into her greeting. Her lovely voice would lift our spirits as she led us in praise songs, and she would often end up dancing around the room. She made the joy of the Lord contagious.

Jane struggled constantly with feelings of rejection. However, no matter how rejected and dejected she felt in her human encounters, she KNEW in her heart that she was completely accepted and loved by her Lord and Savior Jesus. In early 1992, when she lay comatose from a brain virus, her husband brought a cassette player and praise tapes to her hospital room. When she seemed agitated, the music calmed her. Her hand would wave in rhythm. Her expression would grow peaceful. Visitors and nurses kept the music playing almost all the time. When Jane breathed her last labored breath and went home to the Lord, the batteries in her tape player died a few minutes later.

The Tuesday group stopped meeting regularly after that. We didn't break up; we were sent out by the Lord into other relationships. We didn't need to depend on each other any longer. It was time for us to depend on God in new endeavors. We had learned together how to find guidance in God's Word and unload our emotional baggage.

The most important lesson we learned together is this: *Nothing is as important to God as our relationship with him*. Jesus died and rose from the dead to restore our union with God. When we are secure in an intimate bond with our Savior, he quiets all our emotional turmoil with his love.

Chapter 14 Eyegaze: Window Into the Soul

Over the years the Tuesday Group met, I tried to tell Ralph what I was learning about the Lord. I took him and the girls to church on Sundays after we purchased a van in 1980. He always wanted to go, if only to get out of the house once a week. I wished that he could experience the closer intimacy of a small group praying together. I wondered what his relationship with Jesus was like.

About three years after Ralph's brain hemorrhage, someone had prayed that Isaiah 54:4-5 would be true for me. "You will . . . remember no more the reproach of your widowhood. For your Maker is your husband—the Lord Almighty is his name." Everything within me screamed *NO! I have a husband. I want him back.*

I didn't want God to substitute for Ralph, but that began happening as a result of Tuesdays. At the same time, I was learning to love Ralph better, because as we girls drew closer to the Lord, we also worked on our relations with our families, especially husbands and children. We talked about serving our loved ones as though serving the Lord himself. Such an attitude changes the disposition of the server. Consequently, I cared for Ralph more willingly, with more compassion and gentleness, yet an emotional distance remained between us because of his inability to communicate.

Physical separation remained as well. We still had desires. Changing Ralph's external catheter would sometimes bring on a partial erection for him. I felt our lack of sex most strongly at the mid-point of each monthly cycle. Kissing, while still possible was not very appealing, because of Ralph's constant drooling. It was also not medically advisable, because his lack of mobility made him more susceptible to colds. I cried a lot, usually in the shower or alone in my bed—formerly our bed—at night. Having an affair never entered my mind; the thought of another man's hands on my naked body repulsed me. So I prayed, "Lord, you made me with these fluctuating hormones and desires; help me endure them." Years later, menopause made endurance a little easier.

In 1986, we built an addition onto the house, a large first-floor bedroom and a bathroom with a wheel-in shower. Ralph gained privacy for his personal care and we all got our dining room back. I put a single bed in the room next to Ralph's hospital bed and looked forward to spending nights together in the same room if not in the same bed. That lasted about a month. His moaning and the creaking of his bed when he had leg spasms kept me awake. I moved back upstairs and bought a baby monitor to alert me if his moaning grew loud enough to need my attention.

About the same time, a new state program called Attendant Care began. Administered by a non-profit agency, it provided funds for disabled people to hire personal care assistants. The agency helped with paperwork and mediated problems, while allowing the disabled consumer and family to decide who to hire and to supervise their work. Our participation started slowly with just a few hours a week. It was difficult to find reliable workers who could provide the intense level of care that Ralph needed. We were blessed to have three, Maria, Florence, and Doris, who worked with Ralph for more than 20 years, and became part of the family. Many others came and went. Our allotted hours increased to 54 per week in 1992, enabling me to hold a part-time job. As my physical energy declined, I depended increasingly on our helpers.

Our attendant care workers and the many volunteers for Ralph's exercise were obvious blessings from the Lord. Financial help when we needed it was another. Gifts from our church helped outfit our first van with a wheelchair lift. Gifts from family and the labor of Christian friends helped finish the addition to the house. Ralph's Eyegaze Communication System was another of God's gifts. It came to us through a truly supernatural engineering of circumstances.

We first saw the Eyegaze System on a morning TV talk show. The mother of one of Jenny's friends called with the timely tip. She just happened to be home and have her TV on when she would normally have been at work. We had already tried many communication devices controlled by tiny movements like finger twitches or eye blinks. Ralph could not operate any of them consistently. Using the Eyegaze system required only movement of the eye itself, something Ralph could control. A call to the TV network offices in New York gave me the phone number of the developer of this device.

L. C. Technologies was a small company located in Fairfax, Virginia. After talking with a friendly representative who asked many questions about Ralph, I was hopeful the Eyegaze System would work for him. I made a train trip to Washington D.C. to see a demonstration and was further encouraged. When the Eyegaze people brought the System to Philadelphia, I took Ralph to try it.

Donna, a friend who was a speech therapist working with brain-injured people, went along. The trial was disappointing. Ralph had problems using the computer. Donna and I were both discouraged, but the L. C. Tech people were not. They immediately saw ways they could improve the System to make it easier for him to use. Dixon Cleveland, one of the developing engineers, talked to Ralph like a fellow engineer, and thanked him profusely for his helpful input. His wife Nancy, a nurse, talked to Ralph as a person instead of a patient while she adjusted his positioning in front of the computer.

In September 1989, Dixon and Nancy brought an improved Eyegaze System to our home and left it for the weekend while they visited friends in the area. Ralph had two days to play with it. Sunday afternoon, eight friends, including Donna, crowded into his bedroom to watch him use this amazing computer. They were fascinated when he made it say 'hello' and 'how are you?' They cheered with all the enthusiasm of fans at a major sporting event as he played a game of paddleball. They marveled at the possibilities for Ralph, especially after two computer experts tried their hands (or rather their eyes) and found it wasn't as easy as it looked.

The next week, I talked with Donna. She was thrilled with how much more Ralph was able to do this time. Small changes in the System had made a big difference. She asked me about Ralph's reaction to the computer. "Was he able to type how he felt about it?"

"Well," I replied, "he didn't have much time to practice with the typewriter part of the system in the two days we had it, but he was able to spell out his full name and one short phrase."

"What was that? What did he say?" she asked.

"He typed, 'I love you.'"

Donna got a little misty-eyed. "Did he speak it then? Or print it?"

"No," I sighed. "You see, the phone rang, and I was standing there talking on the phone while watching Ralph, and I dropped the phone on the keyboard. It hit the escape key and wiped out everything he had typed." Welcome to the joys and the frustrations of the computer age, Ralph.

After that September weekend with the Eyegaze System, we knew we wanted one. Trouble was it cost nearly $50,000. What happened next is just about miraculous. Our church already had a small "Unks Fund" established for Ralph. After news about the computer appeared in the church newsletter, more donations came in. In November, our pastor, Drew Mann (Jim Bell had retired by then), shared our need with other clergy in town. They decided to donate the offering from the 1989 community Thanksgiving service to the Unks Fund. The local newspaper covered the story, then some not-so-local papers, and then a Philadelphia TV station.

January 2, 1990, Dr. Mann came to our house. He squatted beside Ralph's wheelchair so he could look him in the eye and said, "Ralph, the money's in the bank." A smile began to spread across Ralph's face and became a grin that lasted several minutes. (That is very significant when you remember that he cannot control his facial expressions.) Donations came from strangers in eight states and far exceeded what we needed to purchase the computer. Drew Mann likened it to Jesus' feeding of the five thousand with twelve baskets of leftovers gathered by the disciples. A little over a month later, Dixon Cleveland, who was an old friend by then, delivered Ralph's custom Eyegaze Communication System, L.C. Technologies' system number six.

The next few weeks were exciting as we both learned the System and became proficient at using it. It was also a scary time to me. For twelve years, I had imagined what Ralph would say in various situations based on what he had done and said before his brain injury. I was a little afraid to find out what he really thought. He might not be the same Ralph I knew.

He didn't jump in to writing his memoirs, but was willing to answer questions with short sentences. That's understandable. Pressing keys visually one at a time is still not as easy as talking or as fast as fingers on a keyboard. Commenting on the fund raising effort, he said "PEPLE ARE PRITY WOUDERFUL." He still spells like an engineer. Nothing wrong there.

Then we had our first fight in twelve years. While typing a message, Ralph made a mistake on the last letter of a word. He tried to backspace to fix the letter, but accidentally hit the key above the backspace, creating two mistakes to erase. Since the word he was trying to spell was already obvious without its last letter, I said, "You really don't have to fix that. Just put in a space and go on to the next word."

Ralph hit the backspace, then another wrong key.

I said, "Just go on."

Mistake. Backspace. Backspace.

"Really, Just hit the space bar and start the next word!" I was beginning to sound impatient.

Backspace. Mistake. Backspace. Mistake. Mistake

"Will you please just go on!!"

Backspace.

How long did this exchange continue? I don't know. (Sigh) Who finally won? Ralph did. He stubbornly insisted on erasing until he got that last letter right before he would go to the next word. He was still the same old Ralph.

We took care of practical matters with the computer. Ralph typed "I love you" and "Happy Birthday" to each of the girls on their special day. He rendered opinions on dinner menus and Christmas gifts. He placed calls to relatives with the Eyegaze System's speakerphone; that way he could hear the whole conversation and make the computer speak short comments stored in its memory. He was able to demonstrate to a psychologist and a lawyer that he understood the ramifications of executing a power of attorney. Obtaining that legal document made handling business much easier for me.

For the most part, I avoided asking questions about emotions and faith. When I did ask an open-ended question on an abstract subject, Ralph could only articulate short answers. For example, in response to, "What can you tell about your faith?" he typed, "MY FATH IN GOD IS VERY STRONG." I stopped asking such questions.

Sometimes short statements can speak volumes, however, like when Ralph was demonstrating the Eyegaze System for Jenny's future in-laws (though none of us knew that at the time). There were six or seven people in the room and the place was buzzing with conversation. In response to something somebody said, Ralph typed, "I AM HAPPY ABOUT THAT." By the time he finished the sentence, nobody could remember what had prompted it. I asked him, "Happy about what?" Ralph thought for a long, long time, searching for a word to express what he wanted to say. Others tried to offer suggestions, all of which he ignored. Finally he looked back to the keyboard on the screen and typed, "TO BE ALIVE." Silence fell in the crowded room. Ralph, using only his eyes, had just said, "I AM HAPPY TO BE ALIVE."

Chapter 15 Girls Will Be Girls

Ralph, Jenny and I were sitting at the kitchen table. Jenny had come home from college for the weekend and was filling us in on her life. "I have to do a presentation in psychology next week," she said. "Someone told the professor my Dad is in a wheelchair, and she wants me to talk to the class about what it's like to grow up in a dysfunctional family."

Before I had a chance to comment, Jenny exclaimed indignantly, "Can you believe that? Just because one person in the family can't function physically doesn't mean the family is dysfunctional." She began naming friends with two able-bodied parents and assorted family problems: parents divorced; parents together but fighting all the time; a boy who is a teenage alcoholic; a girl who has threatened suicide. With agitation in her voice, she pronounced her verdict. "Those are dysfunctional! My family functions very well, thank you!"

I had to laugh at Jenny's ranting. Fourteen years earlier, Bernice had tried to dissuade me from bringing Ralph home, convinced that such a move would do irreparable psychological harm to my children. Jenny's comments were invalidating Bernice's fear. I was glad I had chosen the path I had. More recently, as Jenny and I recalled this incident, she quipped, "That psych professor probably did more harm than having a disabled father did. I didn't know my family was dysfunctional until she told me it was."

Jenny majored in special education for the visually impaired and in general elementary education at Kutztown University. She married Steve, a West Point graduate and Army lieutenant, one week after finishing classes at Kutztown. As a fulltime wife and mother, she used her teacher's training daily raising her daughters, Ashley and Kate. In recent years, she has also worked as a pre-Kindergarten teacher. Jenny is effervescent, and enthusiastic about life. She handles the obligations of an officer's wife and the frequent moves with grace. Other military wives and friends often seek her common-sense counsel. Did she gain sensitivity to other's problems and learn how to handle life's crises while growing up in our family? Maybe. Maybe it's the talent and personality she was born with.

Amy has always been quieter than Jenny. In the early months after Ralph's brain hemorrhage, I worried about her, because she did not express her feelings as openly as Jenny. She was always there when I tried to explain what was going on. She cried with Jenny and me. But she didn't say much. When we talk about those days now, she reminds me, "I was only four. I honestly don't remember the details or how I felt."

Years later, my mother told me of an incident she remembered about Amy. Mom and Dad were visiting from Pittsburgh while Ralph was in the hospital. Mom went upstairs one time and found Amy sitting alone in the middle of her parents' bed and looking very thoughtful. She asked, "What're you doing, Amy?" Amy's matter-of-fact reply was, "I liked it better when my Dad was okay." Amy analyzes her own response by saying, "I think that comment indicates I was thinking about the situation and dealing with it, even though I didn't talk about it. I just accepted it and moved on."

As a teenager, Amy developed a passion for classical ballet. We conflicted over what she would do with her life after high school. She wanted to take dance classes in the city and try to get into a professional company. I said you're too smart to be only a dancer; you have to get a college degree so you can support yourself when you're too old to dance. Our compromise solution was a small school more than 500 miles away, Virginia Intermont

College, where she could major in dance with a concentration in classical ballet. An academic scholarship made it *almost* affordable.

Back in Pennsylvania after graduation, Amy spent six years teaching and performing for various studios and dance companies. She then opened her own pre-professional ballet company and school, a non-profit corporation of which she was Artistic Director. For each performance, she choreographed a complete ballet, sometimes with an original story line, compiled the music, designed scenery and costumes, and did much of the sewing herself. The quiet little girl who didn't say much became teacher, director, and business manager, interacting with students of varying ages and abilities, and many different adult personalities.

With the declining economy in 2008, Amy was forced to close her school and has struggled to make a living with various freelance dancing, teaching, and costuming jobs. As director of her company, Amy had immersed herself in the production of fanciful fairy tales, beautifully performed in dance. Did her ardent interest in ballet come about as an escape from the harsh reality of life with disability? Do her fictional dramas reflect a continuing desire to retreat? Some might say so. Maybe it's the talent and personality she was born with.

Both Jenny and Amy had a few problems growing up. They fought with each other. They made messes, usually in the process of being creative. They procrastinated on chores or schoolwork. They fudged the truth or made excuses when they got in trouble. They complained about parental restrictions. In short, they did normal kid stuff. What they did not do is just as significant. Neither of them did drugs or alcohol or 'slept around,' or got arrested. I thank the Lord that he spared me from such problems; I had enough trouble handling normal kid stuff.

My Tuesday Group friends showed me that my kids' problems were not unique to our family situation; they were common to growing up. Marty and Jane often gave good practical advice— wisdom gained through experience, since their children were older than mine. More importantly, they helped me find direction in God's Word. They did not let me turn our times together into kid-bashing sessions. Instead, we prayed for our children and for our own reactions to their problems. We have power to change only our own behavior; it is up to the Holy Spirit to change our children.

What I learned about parenting can be summarized simply: do your best; trust God with the rest; and don't blame yourself for things over which you have no control. I'm sure I did some things right. I tried to be honest with the girls about their father's disabilities without being overly technical. I shared my grief and cried with them. I tried to model acceptance and didn't hide the family situation. We had birthday parties and invited their friends over to play. Ralph went to school plays and band concerts, church choir performances, and dance recitals. I expected the girls to help with age-appropriate household chores. I prayed with them at dinnertime, as they left for school, and when I tucked them in at night. And I encouraged conversation about emotional issues—fears, doubts, and feelings. I'm sure I did a few things wrong as well—like the china cabinet incident.

When Jenny and Amy were in elementary school, Ralph's bedroom was the dining room. The good tableware and linens were in storage. We ate in the kitchen or, when relatives visited, served buffet-style and ate wherever. The living room, also, had been stripped of nonessentials to make space for maneuvering a wheelchair and doing Ralph's exercise. It was our PT gym. The carpeting was worn from the steady traffic of family and helpers. The walls and woodwork were nicked by the wheelchair and other equipment. Only the china cabinet in a corner of the dining room still displayed fine treasures of our former life.

One day, the girls were playing on the floor beside Ralph's bed, wrestling, giggling, rolling around, and acting goofy. From the kitchen, I heard a loud thump and clattering of china and glass. I sprang to the doorway in time to see a knot of young bodies resting against the wooden lower doors of the china cabinet and small objects still toppling behind the glass upper doors. With a shriek, I charged in. The human knot, appearing unhurt, untied itself and separated. I dropped to my knees in front of the china cabinet to inspect the damage. The girls sat silent on the floor watching with fearful looks on their faces.

One of the wooden doors had been jammed inward by the force of the blow. I was able to open the adjacent door and pry the jammed one out. The china inside was unharmed, but the mahogany veneer of the door was chipped. Carefully, I opened the glass doors to avoid having objects resting against them spill out. Gently, lovingly, I inspected each piece and put it back in its place, while lecturing the girls about roughhousing indoors and being careful and respecting property. I started to cry and exclaimed, "I can't keep anything nice around here!" The delicate work my hands were doing contrasted with the tearful tirade coming from my mouth. "Out of the overflow of the heart the mouth speaks" (Matthew 12:34). Obviously, the god I was worshiping on my knees in front of the china cabinet was not Jesus.

Recalling the incident, Jenny says, "We were just praying that you wouldn't find anything broken, because we knew we'd really get it then." Thankfully, nothing was broken—at least nothing material. Family peace was broken and our relations strained for a time. No glass or china was lost, but I lost forever one opportunity to teach about God's love, forgiveness, and values. Chipped veneer remains to remind me of that. The girls learned to love, forgive, and value godly virtues anyway. God also provided material blessings for them in many wonderful ways.

When Amy was four and Jenny six, a friend gave them introductory piano lessons. They had obvious interest and apparent talent for music, so I prayed about whether or not to invest in a piano and commit to lessons. I was learning to seek guidance in Scripture, and the Spirit led me to Psalms. The words of Psalm 33 stood out for me. "Sing joyfully to the Lord, you righteous; it is fitting for the upright to praise him. Praise the Lord with the harp; make music to him on the ten-stringed lyre. Sing to him a new song; play skillfully and shout for joy" (Psalm 33:1-3). God seemed to be saying, "Yes, buy the piano, and begin lessons for the girls; they will praise me in song."

The Lord confirmed his word as I began to act on it. He helped me find a second-hand piano that fit into our living room *and* our budget. He led us to a series of excellent Christian teachers who included hymns and praise music in their lessons. After many years of instruction and hundreds of hours of practice, he gave both girls opportunities to play at church to "Praise the Lord with the harp." The Lord fulfilled his prophecy.

When Jenny and Amy were about ten and twelve, they were learning dances from Tchaikovsky's Nutcracker in their ballet classes. The time seemed right for them to appreciate a live professional ballet. One day, after hearing an advertisement on the radio, I silently wondered (only wondered) if I could take them to see the Nutcracker at Christmas time when visiting relatives would be here to stay with Ralph. Minutes later (yes, minutes), Norma called. She and her husband Al had no children and she wondered if they could borrow ours to see the Nutcracker. "Before a word is on my tongue you know it completely, O Lord" (Psalm139:4).

Ralph and I always enjoyed camping in the woods beside a quiet lake. We took the girls when they were babies, but not anymore. So I assumed. Our friends Ed and Karen thought differently and invited us to visit their cottage on a tiny island in the middle of a lake. I had seen pictures of their cottage. It looked about as accessible as Alcatraz, but Ed and Karen kept asking and kept assuring us that it really was possible. Several years after the original offer, I finally said yes.

We arrived on the wooded shore of Beaver Lake in mid-afternoon on a rainy summer Saturday. If it had not been for the girls' excited urging, I would have turned around and gone back home when we hit the first cloudburst in our three-hour journey. Ed, Karen, and their sons, Chris and Jon, met us at the dock in an outboard motorboat just big enough for the four of them, two eight-foot planks, and a pile of rain ponchos.

"We're doomed," I thought.

Reading my dubious expression, Ed said, with a twinkle in his eye, "Don't worry, Nancy!" He dropped the planks on the shore and disappeared into a covered boathouse nearby. The four kids began plotting their weekend adventures, undaunted by the dampness.

Ed soon reappeared on the water at the helm of a motorized barge. At least that's what he called it. It was a plywood platform, about 8 feet wide and 12 feet long mounted on steel drums and powered by a chugging, coughing, smoking outboard motor. There were no side rails, and I could see large rust holes in two of the steel drums. Ed guided this contraption into position by a pier and tossed ropes to Karen and the boys.

"It's gonna work, Nancy," he said. "Don't worry."

To my amazement, it did. The planks formed a bridge to get Ralph and his wheelchair from the pier to the barge and then from the barge to the island dock. Then, they became a ramp over steps into the cottage, where the aroma of hot soup simmering on the stove greeted us. Once we found our beds and unpacked, the kids disappeared to tour the island. There was nothing for me to do but sit around and eat (and feed Ralph, of course) until bedtime. How heavenly!

Sunday dawned clear and sunny. The four kids spent the day on or in the lake. Once Ralph was dressed and in his wheelchair, I again had only to sit, eat, and enjoy the scenery. That evening, as we packed to board the barge (which, Ed had told us, was the community garbage scow) for our return trip, we were already talking about "next year."

I praise God for these friends who would not take 'no' for an answer. They pursued us until we came, just as God's Spirit pursues us until we draw close to him. They carried us over the stormy water, made a safe path for our feet (or wheels), fed us, sheltered us, and entertained us. Beaver Lake became an annual tradition until the kids were all out of high school. Our girls never got bored with it; they loved exploring inlets and swamps by canoe, inventing pirate games with their "brothers," swimming from island to island, hiking forest trails, and observing wildlife. Those trips gave them many stories for the annual what-I-did-with-my-summer-vacation essay in English class, and some of their classmates were truly envious.

Jenny and Amy did not miss many advantages while growing up. They had creative toys; we would have nixed gimmicky junk anyway. They had stylish clothes—not the hottest funky fads, but stylish. (I discovered early that it was better to buy them two pairs of brand-name jeans that they would wear over and over than to spend the same amount of money on six pairs of cheap jeans that they hated.) They experienced amusement parks and museums. They even went to Disney World when friends took them along as baby-sitters for their preschoolers. Two years later, Amy went again with the high school band.

A few months after Ralph got his Eyegaze System, Jenny went to her first prom. On prom day, she asked Dad what time she had to be in. I was thinking of a time that I knew was earlier than her friends' curfews. Ralph typed a time an hour earlier than mine. Jenny's mouth dropped open, and I braced for the protest. Then she closed it and brightly said, "Okay." She told all of her friends what time *Dad* said she had to be in, and she was home with a few minutes to spare.

Perhaps one opportunity the girls missed was the chance to observe positive interaction between a husband and wife. Again, the Lord provided. When Jenny was in college, Marty and John retired to a mountain retreat about half an hour's drive from Kutztown. During her last semester on campus, Jenny lived with them and commuted over the mountain to class each day. She was engaged to Steve at the time and fully appreciated the role model that Marty and John provided in their relationship. She commented, "I hope Steve and I can be such good friends when we have been married that long." So far, they seem to be succeeding.

Yes, the Lord has provided what the girls needed when they needed it. I didn't always rest in peace and confidence that he would come through. Sometimes I objected to what he was trying to do—for example, Beaver Lake. I did more worrying than necessary. Too often, I shouldered blame for their problems and tried to solve them myself. Because of Jesus, I can now rest in the knowledge that I did my best. Whatever may still be lacking in my children's training for life, he will yet provide. After all, he's still working on me.

Chapter 16 Seeking Healing

As I drove homeward down Route 309, my eyes automatically scanned the landscape. Ahead, the highway arched up into the sky and curved gently left. On the right below the road, open fields spread toward the western horizon. A low sun, shrouded in late summer haze, gave a yellow glow to the scene, while above the fields a hawk soared in wide, lazy circles.

I glanced in the rear-view mirror. The tops of the girls' blonde heads were visible on opposite sides of the van's way-back seat. Jenny's head faced the window; Amy's nodded toward the center. I surmised that Jenny was watching the scenery, and Amy was probably almost asleep. Typical. In the middle of the van, between the girls and me, I saw Ralph's head and shoulders strapped into his wheelchair. He was hunched to the right, eyes closed, right fist drawn up to his chin, a frown of pain on his face. Also typical. It had been a long day, and *nothing* had changed.

In my mind, I envisioned the hawk's eye view of us. Our little brown, tan, and white van moved slowly along the highway—55-mph seeming more like 5-mph from the sky. The people inside were invisible, the horizon expansive. Suddenly, I saw a greater picture: God's hand of protection over our van and its tired driver. We were not invisible to God, though his horizons are limitless. I made a silent vow never to subject my family or myself to the disappointment of another healing service. "Lord, you hear my own prayers for Ralph's healing. If you want to use other people to bring it about, you can send them to us. You know where we live. We don't ever have to make a trip like this again."

That was the last of many such pilgrimages. While our church was under an interim pastor after Jim Bell's retirement in 1979, we explored other churches where healing is openly preached and practiced. We went to see several well-known evangelists when they came to the Philadelphia area. We listened to tapes of healing Scriptures and watched The 700 Club. I say 'we' because I did consult Ralph about whether or not he wanted to do these things. He always gave a hopeful 'yes' response. If he wanted to try it, how could I deny him that chance?

The girls had no choice. They were eight and six when we got our first van in 1980 and began our odysseys in search of a miracle. They were good passengers, though. They took along notebooks and pens and drew pictures during the services, tuning out most of the preaching. In fact, they were so tuned-out that when we went back to our old church after a new pastor arrived, the girls completely missed his children's sermons for the first two weeks.

The lessons learned on our quest were valuable. The preachers did not limit their sermons to one short text at a time, so I quickly became familiar with the whole Bible. In the process, I memorized much Scripture. Music was another plus. In Charismatic services, we had our introduction to contemporary worship music. With catchy tunes and a passion for Jesus, their uplifting words were easy to remember and sing.

I learned more about the Holy Spirit. We saw manifestations of the Spirit, which seemed legitimate—speaking in tongues, singing and dancing in the Spirit, falling under the power, prophesying. I also learned that these actions can be ritualized, abused, or faked just as piety is in formal churches.

I learned to pray in the Spirit, in tongues, when talking privately to God. The Apostle Paul acknowledges using tongues that way: "For anyone who speaks in a tongue does not speak to men but to God" (1 Corinthians 14:2). The practice helps me focus on the Lord—his love, his holiness, his glory. The first English words that come to mind after that are usually words of praise. I am bringing the situation to God and praising him. By doing so, I get my desires out of the way so God can answer the prayer his way.

Obviously, we found that not everyone who seeks healing receives it. Continual exposure to faith teaching began to put guilt on us; there must be something wrong with our faith, our prayers, or us. We were ostracized by others. Pursuit of healing distracted our attention from Jesus. We lost sight of the fact that to God, spiritual health and eternal salvation are much more important than temporary physical well-being. We are, after all, mortal.

In pursuit of healing, I also learned how to recognize and avoid cults. At one independent fellowship, the gifts of the Spirit flowed. Then the pastor moved to another state, calling his own replacement. The new pastor had apparent psychological problems, including an enormous lust for food. His wife wore long skirts, long sleeves and a scarf on her head all year. Other women in the church began to follow.

There were deeper problems. A woman gave a damning prophecy about the church. She was ushered out and never came back. A baby died because his parents looked to God alone for his healing. When they finally rushed him to a hospital, it was too late. Educated professional people began to leave the congregation, and the pastor warned about associating with those who had left.

I sensed that something was very wrong. "Lord, I can't just run away," I prayed. "Lead us to a new place and, please, confirm it in your Word." That week, I ran into a friend from our old church and thought it would be nice to visit there again. Ralph was all for it.

Sunday morning, we pulled into the familiar parking lot and were greeted with warm enthusiasm. The welcome continued inside. Pastor Drew Mann's sermon was the Biblical confirmation I had asked for. It was about tearing down the many artificial walls we build between friends, families, races, and denominations. Jesus died on the cross to tear down the greatest wall of all, the wall of sin that separates us from God. I had built an artificial wall by thinking churches that practiced healing had more truth.

God seemed to be leading us back home, but I wanted to be sure. The next week we returned to the independent fellowship. Again, I prayed that God would confirm in his Word our intended move. During a rambling teaching on Romans, the pastor digressed into criticizing mainstream churches. Looking straight at me, he likened going back to a denominational church with the Israelites going back to captivity in Babylon.

As he continued, my eyes fell on Romans 2:1. "You, therefore, have no excuse, you who pass judgement on someone else, for at whatever point you judge the other, you are condemning yourself, because you who pass judgement do the same things." The week before, we had heard about tearing down walls. This pastor persisted in building walls by his critical spirit. "Thank you, Jesus," I whispered. The Lord had confirmed in his Word the direction we were to go.

During the following week, I anticipated our return to our old Presbyterian Church. I wanted to tell friends there what we had learned about healing, but the Lord impressed on me that I should simply show up on Sunday mornings and smile. So, that's what I did for the next ten years. Nobody asked where we had been during our absence. Apparently, they thought we were too emotionally distraught over Ralph's condition to come to church. They welcomed us back into the fold and blessed us in many ways.

We continued to pray for healing. The Bible instructs us to do so. "Is any one of you sick? He should call the elders of the church to pray over him and anoint him with oil in the name of the Lord. And the prayer offered in faith will make the sick person well; the Lord will raise him up. If he has sinned, he will be forgiven" (James 5:14-15). We left the answer in God's hands. If we could control God, then he would not be God and would not be worthy of our worship.

While Ralph and I continued praying for a big miracle, we did see several smaller healings as a result of prayer. One was Ralph's survival of the initial brain hemorrhage with his mind intact. While many people prayed for him, he had gradually improved to the point where he could live at home. He was reasonably healthy and free from the pressure sores, urinary tract infections, and pneumonia that are common for quadriplegics.

During an uncommon bout with a nasty urinary infection in 1992, we discovered that Ralph cannot take the class of antibiotics usually prescribed for such problems; for him they have dangerous neurological side effects. We spent five months trying various less potent drugs with little improvement, and then one day the infection was gone. The only possible explanation is that God intervened in answer to prayer. Through that experience, we saw how blessed we were that God maintained Ralph's general health.

Cramps in his legs were Ralph's most bothersome ongoing problem. Many people prayed with us for relief. The Lord's answer was to lead us to alleviating medical treatments. Muscle relaxing drugs seemed to help for a while, but we eventually rejected them because they had undesirable side effects. In 1992, Ralph had surgery to implant an electrical stimulator on the spinal cord. The impulses helped relax his legs. Ten years later, it did not seem to work anymore. In fact, it was having the opposite effect, so we stopped using it.

In 1999 and 2000, Ralph had surgeries on his feet to correct the painful deformities that had been caused by years of spasticity. Our old friends, Nancy and Hank, who continued to care for their son Fred at home, had told us about the orthopedic surgeon who performed these procedures. Fred had his hand straightened the same day Ralph had his first foot surgery. Nancy, Hank, and I had a happy hospital reunion, sharing what the Lord had done for us over twenty years. We agreed that we don't seek medical miracles any more, only treatments that relieve pain and increase comfort.

Proponents of various radical cures had tempted us in the past. When Ralph first came home from the hospital, several people urged us to do an intensive therapy program called patterning, which involves putting the patient through the motions of crawling several times a day. The technique is purported to have had amazing results with brain-injured children. However, Ralph was an adult. His tense, rigid muscles made it difficult even to do range-of-motion therapy designed to stretch and relax. Basic care and feeding took up so much of our day that adding patterning would leave no time for anything else. We decided against the program.

Many years later, a friend who had been assisting with Ralph's range-of-motion tried to talk us into another patterning-type program, offering to pay for the evaluation. I read the literature to Ralph and gave him the choice. I was relieved when Ralph again rejected the plan in favor of spending his time using his Eyegaze Communication System, listening to talking books, watching TV, and being entertained by the girls. I told the friend that if he could find anyone as old as Ralph who had been as severely handicapped for as long as Ralph and yet benefited from this kind of therapy, then we would try it. Unfortunately, we lost a friend over the issue, but we did not regret our decision.

By then, we had grown in our faith. Healing for the earthly body no longer seemed so important in view of the resurrection body we would someday receive with Jesus in heaven. We had found peace with Jesus, our healer. The further pursuit of miracles, by faith or medicine, seemed only to upset that peace. We were not quite ready to go along with Job and say, "Though he slay me, yet will I hope in him" (Job 13:15). At least, I wasn't. Maybe Ralph was.

Chapter 17 Finding Health

Ralph has taught me more about the Holy Spirit than all of our
ventures into the Charismatic world did. While he was in the
hospital in 1978, I was just discovering the Spirit and trying to
understand him. I wrote to Ralph, "I can't live any more with
gloom, pessimism, fear, and doubt. I have to let the hope of the
Lord Jesus Christ live in me. It's only with that hope, that Spirit,
that I have the energy to give you the encouragement and love
you need."

Two times stand out in my memory when I missed the Spirit.
One was during the depression that ensued after I began to
realize the permanency of Ralph's disabilities. I wrote, "without
the Spirit during my weeks of depression, I was in hell." The other

time was after Ralph came home. The miracle I had hoped for
wasn't happening. Therapy wasn't going well. I told God, "You're
not helping. Get out of my life!" Weeks followed when everything
went wrong, until I begged God, "Please come back."

How did I know the absence of the Spirit was hell? As I wrote
to Ralph, "Whether I'm aware if its presence or not, when I am
without the Spirit, it is just like the times when we had a fight and
I felt that I was without your love. I lived in hell until we made up
or until I let the spirit of your love back into my life. Thank God he
gave me your love to teach me how to recognize the love of his
Holy Spirit."

Near the end of my long letter, I had offered a prayer-like plea
for the Spirit to fill Ralph. Apparently, God answered. Ten years
later, Ralph received a talking book in the mail from the library.
The title was intriguing: *Where Is God When It Hurts?* Not knowing
anything about the book or its author, Philip Yancey, I was wary.
Would it debunk faith or encourage it? We listened together, and
I questioned Ralph about his reaction at every break. Each time,
with a hand squeeze or a grunt, he indicated agreement. Where *is*
God when life hurts? Right here with us in the midst of the pain.
We had spent ten years coming to the same conclusion that the
book stated so eloquently. We had sought healing but found
health in Jesus, the healer.

A healthy faith had been growing through Ralph's example and my Tuesday Group friends, but the Spirit had more to teach me. I was only beginning to discern his leading in everyday situations, and I had much to learn about trusting him to solve my problems. So, the Lord arranged for me to work as Christian Education Director for our church from 1992 until 1999. The job was ideal. Part-time flexible hours allowed me to do much of the work at home. It was an opportunity to give back to the church that had given so much to us. Besides, the pay was welcome. With the girls in college, financial needs were greater than ever while the budget was tighter.

Through planning lessons, teaching, and writing for the church newsletter, I learned more about the Bible. God often spoke to me regarding my own life in lessons I prepared for children. The constant recruiting of teachers was not my favorite part of the job, but it was part of the Holy Spirit's lesson plan for me. I learned to trust him to lead me to the right people at the right time. I came to recognize his voice—a silent nudge in the back of my mind indicating, "Speak now; the time is right."

In the spring of 1992, soon after I started the church job, my Dad had a paralyzing stroke. Dad and Mom needed my help in Pittsburgh. Ralph needed me at home. I was torn. By then Florence and Maria had both been Ralph's attendants for a few years, and Jenny and Amy were old enough to be responsible for the house, so I arranged a two-day trip as soon as possible. Heading west on the turnpike, I played a new tape of praise music. Somewhere around Harrisburg, the Spirit spoke through words from a song, calming my fears about what I would find and how I would handle it. He told me, "God will make a way where there seems to be no way."

God did indeed make the way over the next two years as I juggled Ralph's care, a new job, many short trips to Pittsburgh, and the needs of two kids in college. After Jenny and Steve's wedding in 1994, I concentrated on arranging to bring Mom and Dad to a life-care retirement home nearby. That way I could monitor their daily care, freeing my brother to handle cleaning out and selling their house. In September, we made the move.

With Mom and Dad only ten minutes away, it was easy to visit them often. All that I had learned about brain injuries by caring for Ralph helped me understand and communicate with Dad, so I could be his advocate with the nursing center staff. It was a privilege to be with him when he died in September 1996. By then, Mom had begun having her own health problems and had had breast cancer surgery about four months earlier. She, too, was glad they had moved across the state when they did. We could see that the timing was God's work. Looking back on that "sandwich generation" period in my life, I am amazed that I was able to deal with so many happenings at once. The strength and sanity could only have come from the Holy Spirit.

By 1998, my family responsibilities had lessened. The nest was empty. Our first granddaughter, Ashley, lived 300 miles away, but her parents brought her to visit every three or four months. In the meantime, I thoroughly enjoyed my work with the children at church. However, when the part-time youth leader left, church officers decided to seek an associate pastor who would do both youth work and Christian education. Thus, my job would end. Disappointed at first, I later began to look forward to "retirement" and having more time to write. I could finish the story of what Jesus has done for us through Ralph's brain hemorrhage.

That summer, I was asked to give a sermon when the minister would be on vacation. I sensed the now familiar nudge from the Holy Spirit, and said yes. I knew what my topic must be and what Bible text I would use. I had to tell my story—my testimony—to tell them that, because of Jesus, no tragedy can separate us from the love of God. The time for simply going to church and smiling had passed. The time for teaching the kids had passed. It was time to speak to the adults about what Jesus will do for anyone who comes to him.

To write that speech, I had to go back in memory to events I would rather forget—the events of the early chapters in this book. I had to admit publicly my fears and doubts, my sins of unbelief and my lack of trust. The 20-minute talk was carefully rehearsed. While speaking from the pulpit, I saw a few people discreetly dabbing their eyes, but I kept my cool. I concluded by inviting people to ask Jesus to be their Savior and Lord. Then, I read the reassuring verses of Romans 8:35-39.

While facing those friends and supporters in August 1998, the Spirit nudged again. I felt a sense of finality—that this telling of our story was both a first and a last. The Lord seemed to be saying, "Your work is done here. I'm going to move you on." I did not want to believe that. For another year, I continued to administer the Sunday school program and organize things for my unknown successor. During that time, I kept asking the Lord, "Where do we go next?" and "Why?" The Spirit was silent.

When duty no longer demanded my presence, we visited other churches. Ralph was open to change, and I counted on his yea-or-nay input to confirm or check my interpretation of the Spirit's leading. We tried three churches and were drawn unmistakably to one that is part of a different Presbyterian denomination. Together, we agreed to alternate Sundays between the new church and our old one. Surprisingly, after one more visit, Ralph indicated with a hand squeeze that he wanted to attend the new church regularly. His choice confirmed my own feeling. The Spirit did seem to be leading us there, but I still did not know why.

At New Life Church, we were welcomed into a home group. It was Ralph's first-ever chance to be part of a small Bible study and prayer group. Half the participants were men, a nice change from the female caregivers who usually surrounded him. We were the senior members. Everyone else was at least 15 years younger. We found their energy refreshing. They found our faith inspiring, though we didn't say much. We just came and enjoyed the fellowship. In Sunday morning worship, the music and Bible teaching seemed to speak to me personally, encouraging me to spend more time in God's Word.

The time came to make a decision about which church to call home. Ralph seemed to have made up his mind: New Life. I vacillated. What would people think? Would we lose friends? Didn't we have an obligation to the old church? They still held the "Unks Fund" for Ralph's Eyegaze System and other special needs. Would they think we were ungrateful? Would they think I was angry about losing my job? Or that I'd had a major disagreement with somebody? What would people think?

All of my reservations were about people, not about God. The "fear of man" was controlling me instead of the "fear of God." I knew I should move ahead with the Spirit. Instead, I was looking back longingly on comfort, tradition, and public opinion. I talked with the pastor and some elders at our old church. They seemed understanding. We reached an agreement that the Unks Fund would remain for its intended purpose. Ralph and I joined New Life Presbyterian Church. However, doubt kept gnawing, especially when I ran into someone from the old church in the supermarket. The doubts finally stopped in February of 2001, when we gave our testimony in front of the new church.

Mike, our home group leader and a pastoral assistant, asked me to do a 3-minute talk telling how Ralph and I had come to faith in Jesus. My twenty-minute sermon at the other church told only my side of the story. It seemed impossible to condense it into three minutes and include Ralph's faith, too. But the Holy Spirit said, "Do it," so I started writing. When I got our story down to twelve minutes, I emailed it to Mike, who showed it to pastor Ron, who said, "The congregation needs to hear this."

Three times our testimony was scheduled and snowed out. On a rainy Sunday near the end of February, God's timing was right. I took Ralph up front with me when I spoke and demonstrated how I take his hand to get his response to questions. Members of our home group, sitting near the front, said they had never seen Ralph smile so much. Pastor Ron, in his sermon, referred to our story as a message of encouragement pointing people to the gospel of Jesus Christ. It was Ralph's part of the story that was most compelling. Here it is:

"What about Ralph's viewpoint? Ralph has an Eyegaze Computer System, which lets him communicate using the only muscles he can control reliably—the tiny muscles that move his right eyeball. On several occasions he has spelled out, 'God is very hard on me.' When he first said that, I read lots of Scripture and theology to him, and tried to assure him that God loves him and is not punishing him. Still he typed the same message. Over weeks and months of this exchange, he indicated that, yes, he *knows* in his mind God loves him, but he doesn't always *feel* it. I asked him, 'What would help you feel more like God loves you?' He spelled out, 'If I didn't hurt so much.'

"You see, even when you are not actively using your muscles, your brain is constantly sending them messages telling them to relax. When your brain is not fully in control, muscles do things by themselves. They go into spasms and cramp up. Cramps are very painful. Repeated spasms and cramping over time actually deform joints, especially between the small bones of the feet and hands. This adds more pain.

"That's what Ralph has experienced for nearly twenty-three years. The daily exercise we do for him, with the assistance of volunteers, helps relieve the cramping, but it cannot undo or prevent the damage his own muscles do to his body the other 23½ hours of the day. Our constant prayer is for relief from the pain. In the past two years, we have seen the best answers yet to that prayer through surgeries to correct the foot deformities and nerve blocking injections, which temporarily reduce the muscle spasms.

"About a year and a half ago, a friend gave me the book, *When God Weeps* by Joni Eareckson Tada and Steven Estes. Joni is a quadriplegic and Steve an ordained minister. Together they tackle the problem of pain and suffering from the perspective of one who has lived it and from the Bible. It is a very readable treatment of a tough theological issue. After I finished it, I began reading it to Ralph.

"In the book, Joni makes the statement: 'I would rather be in this [wheel] chair knowing [Jesus] than on my feet without him.'[3] When I read that part to Ralph, I stopped. I was not sure I could agree with her if I were the one suffering. I asked Ralph, 'What do you think? Do you agree, disagree, or would like to agree but you're not there yet?'

"I re-read the paragraph, put my hand into Ralph's right hand, and repeated my three choices. When I said, 'Squeeze if you agree with Joni's statement,' he immediately squeezed long and hard. I was surprised. It was not what I expected him to pick. Besides, I usually don't get a response that strong when I give him a choice of desserts, his favorite part of any meal.

---

[3] Joni Eareckson Tada and Steven Estes, *When God Weeps: Why Our Sufferings Matter to the Almighty*, (Grand Rapids, MI: Zondervan Publishing House, 1997), 181.

"Despite the pain, I would rather be in this wheelchair knowing Jesus than on my feet without him. What can I add to that loudly spoken hand squeeze? It seems appropriate for God's word to have the final say here. The last few verses of the eighth chapter of Romans have had special meaning for us for many years. I like the way the passage is paraphrased in *The Message* by Eugene Peterson:

'Do you think anyone is going to be able to drive a wedge between us and Christ's love for us? There is no way! Not trouble, not hard times, not hatred, not hunger, not homelessness, not bullying threats, not backstabbing, not even the worst sins listed in scripture... None of this fazes us because Jesus loves us. I'm absolutely convinced that nothing—nothing living or dead, angelic or demonic, today or tomorrow, high or low, thinkable or unthinkable—absolutely nothing can get between us and God's love because of the way that Jesus our Master has embraced us.'[4]"

As I placed the microphone back in its stand, I saw people weeping openly. Again, the Spirit nudged, "This is the place for you now—the place where you will be embraced by Jesus." God confirmed that word in reality. We grew closer to Jesus. We enjoyed small-group fellowship, and a group began meeting in our home. We were inspired by the testimonies of others. We saw our

---

[4] Eugene H. Peterson, *The Message: The New Testament in Contemporary English*, (Colorado Springs CO: NavPress Publishing Group, 1993), 320.

volunteer roster revitalized with younger helpers, some of whom challenged us with the maturity of their faith.

Dave and Ashley came to help with Ralph's exercise on Saturday mornings for a couple of years. They had grown up and married in New Life Church, and they spoke easily about their faith. We were excited for them when they told us they were expecting their first child. Then, in April 2002, two weeks before Ashley's due date, Dave was diagnosed with non-Hodgkin's Lymphoma. We gasped with the entire congregation when Pastor Ron made the announcement. He called Dave and Ashley up front, where the elders laid hands on them and prayed.

I remembered when we were a young couple with a devastating diagnosis. Feelings of futility crept into my heart as we prayed for Dave's healing. After the service, Dave asked if he could give our names to their friend Sandy, who was organizing an email prayer letter. He said they really wanted us to pray for them. "Sure," I said while thinking, "*Why?*" James 5:15 says, "The prayer offered in faith will make the sick person well." I didn't feel my faith was strong enough to get a hangnail healed, let alone cancer.

Over the ensuing months, we followed Dave and Ashley's lives through Sandy's frequent email updates, including treatment reports, specific prayer requests, and pictures of Layne, their beautiful little daughter. Six months later, all tests showed Dave to be cancer free! Just as remarkable is the fact that his treatment side effects were minimal, and he continued to work throughout that time.

What challenged me was Dave's number one request in the very first prayer letter in April: "That God would be glorified through all of this!" His number two request was, "That our faith would be strengthened." Cure of the cancer was only number four on his list. In December, after their cancer-free news, Sandy wrote, "God has carried their family through such an ordeal with amazing examples of His love and care for them along the way. He has sustained their peace during a time that could have been fearful and anxious, and He has kept their faith strong at a time when they could have doubted. I know they are so grateful that you have been praying for them, and they see tangible evidence of those prayers all over!"

I said in chapter five that I am skeptical of stories about Christians who persevere through incredible trials with unwavering faith. Dave and Ashley proved me wrong. They experienced extreme emotions and temptations to doubt and fear. They continued to deal with the possibility that cancer would return or that some delayed treatment side effects would manifest. However, their faith in God and his love for them did not wane. God has been glorified through their continuing story. I am grateful to have been part of their "prayer team" and to have witnessed their inspiring drama. God knew I needed that. While they were going through cancer in 2002, I was in the middle of two most difficult years.

Chapter 18 New Millennium Drought

In eastern Pennsylvania, the first two years of the twenty-first century were ones of record low rainfall. However, in May of 2001, we did not know a two-year drought was beginning. We were just enjoying beautiful, warm, sunny spring weather. We had to water newly planted flowers, but that was normal. By August of 2002, we had given up on flowers, and fifty-year-old trees were dropping their leaves under heat stress.

For me, it was a time of spiritual drought as well. Life left little time to water the soul with God's Word. I raced from one task to the next without ever opening the Bible, breathing hurried prayers of "Help!" My longest conversations with God were questions, "What next? What else can go wrong?" Then, "Please don't answer that one, Lord." Sometimes a remembered scripture verse would offer a little comfort. Maybe I would hear something relevant in a worship song or sermon. It was only a bucket-full of water dumped at the base of a heat-stressed tree.

In May 2001, I didn't know I was heading into that drought. I was enjoying the sunny promise of new blessings from the Lord emerging like spring bulbs. Our attendant care and volunteer help had been slowly diminishing over the past year, but surely, *surely* new people would fill those voids soon. I was looking forward to two short vacations in June, and making plans for Ralph's care in my absence. One trip would be to Baltimore for a reunion with some college friends I had not seen in more than thirty years. The other would be a train trip to Boston to visit Jenny, Steve, Ashley, and Katie.

Mother's day weekend brought more promise. Friday, Amy called and made an "appointment" to come and talk to us about "something important." She was living several miles away with friends, and her busy dance-teaching schedule took her in the opposite direction, so we didn't see much of her. She came in looking serious, sad, and nervous. I wheeled Ralph into the living room where we could all sit comfortably.

"What's on your mind?" I asked.

"I've been really sad lately and I'm seeing a counselor."

I waited. Amy explained how her sadness had become too much for her in the past two weeks and how she had gone to a counselor friend about it. "One of the things we are going to be working on," she said, "is eating."

"Praise the Lord," I exclaimed softly. Besides her Bachelor of Arts degree, Amy had come home from college with eating disorders. My pleas for her to get professional help and her refusal had driven a wedge between us.

Amy continued talking. I listened and made short comments of encouragement. Her counselor felt moving would help her get away from some negative influences. Hesitantly, I proffered the suggestion that she could move back home. We agreed to consider it. I hugged her hard before she left.

After church on Sunday, Amy met us at Mom's retirement home for Mother's Day dinner. Later, she came back to our house and we talked about details of her possible move. It would be difficult, but there could be mutual benefit. We agreed to proceed.

Every spare minute for the next two weeks, I worked on preparing room for Amy. The large bedroom she and Jenny shared as kids had to be completely emptied, because she was moving back with her own furniture. I praised the Lord for his answer to years of prayer for Amy and for the promise of help for me. I rejoiced in the idea of having another able-bodied adult in the house. I had been feeling more tired and, well, older. A glance at the calendar confirmed the age thing; it was full of doctor's appointments for my over-fifty maintenance, as well as the usual ones for Ralph and Mom.

Amy moved in on Memorial Day in the rain. She was here to oversee the household while I went to Baltimore the next weekend. On Saturday afternoon, June 16, I set out to take Ralph and Mom to see Amy and her ballet students perform. That was the day tropical storm Allison struck. What should have been a pleasant ride in the country turned out to be a nightmare odyssey through a torrential downpour, flooded roads, and detours. Responsibility for my two handicapped passengers added stress. We didn't get home until midnight. The next significant rainfall would not come until autumn of 2002, nearly a year and a half later. Memories of that treacherous trip haunted me as problems piled up in the summer and fall of 2001. My spiritual drought commenced.

The first week wasn't bad. Monday, I took Mom for her mammogram and a check-up with her oncologist. She had a good report; her next appointment would be in four months instead of three. It was a welcome step of progress since her breast cancer surgery five years before. After that, I enjoyed my trip to Boston, despite the stress of preparing detailed instructions for Ralph's care, attempting to anticipate *anything* that could possibly go wrong. It was after I got back that things started to go wrong.

Visiting Mom one day in July, I bent down to kiss her goodbye and noticed a bump on her forehead.

"What did you do to your head?" I asked.

"I don't know."

"You have a lump here. It looks like you bumped it except it's not black and blue. We'd better show it to the nurse."

I did an about face and marched down the hallway to the nurse's office. Mom shuffled after, pushing her walker, her "trusty steed," which she had nicknamed "Silver." She began a new round of doctor appointments and tests. In September, a biopsy of the lump showed that it was metastasized breast cancer. More tests in October checked Mom's whole body for other possible cancer sites.

I called my cousin Carolyn. Her father is Mom's brother, my Uncle John. Carolyn and I had a tradition of bringing Mom and Uncle John together to celebrate their October birthdays. This year the birthday party, October 18, seemed more important than ever. On October 30th, I took Mom to the oncologist to hear the test results and treatment options. Chemotherapy appointments were set up for every other week and began that day.

October 31st, I got a call from my niece, Beth, in Pittsburgh. As soon as I heard her voice, I knew it was bad news. My brother, Bob, was having emergency surgery the next day to repair a leaking heart valve. On Halloween night, I prayed with him by phone in his hospital room. Tears streamed down my face, and from the catch in his voice, I suspect Bob was misty-eyed himself. Afterward, I had to call Mom with the news. November commenced with frequent calls to Beth and my sister-in-law, Mary, and to Bob, when he was able to talk again. He came through surgery well, but nearly died from an infection two weeks later.

Meanwhile, life with Amy had not fulfilled my expectations or hers. I could see no progress on her eating problems. She wasn't around much when I needed help. Regarding housekeeping, we were a classic Oscar/Felix *Odd Couple* duo. She quit counseling, and made plans to move out. On November 11, she moved into her own apartment much closer to her job and twenty miles away from us. I felt abandoned.

Attendant care help for Ralph was at an all-time low. Most weekends, we had none. One of our long time attendants, Florence, was having shoulder and neck pain and had to cut down her hours during the week as well. In fact, we were looking for someone to replace her for a much-needed sabbatical. But it wasn't happening.

Then, the holidays were upon us. Thanksgiving. Christmas. New Years. Nice family togetherness times. More work. More stress. The one hopeful spot: December 5, Pastors Mike and Ron met with Amy and me to help us begin working out our differences. With their help, we made a little progress in restoring our relationship. While Amy struggled alone with her eating, it was easier for me to trust God to help her when I did not have to watch day-to-day problems. I prayed that God would bless her and protect her. But I still worried.

My feelings of hurt and abandonment continued. I had hoped Amy would fill the void in our shortage of human helpers. I should have trusted God. I *said* I trusted him to help my daughter. Why couldn't I have the same confidence that he would help me? The daily grind was overwhelming me—cooking, laundry, household chores, home repairs, static revenue, rising expenses, Ralph's constant physical needs, and my ever-present stuffy nose and headaches, which persisted in spite of sinus surgery two years earlier.

Monday morning, January 14, 2002, I retreated to the small upstairs bedroom that is my office. It was the first "free" morning I had had in months. With Bible, legal pad, pen, and a cozy throw, I sank into a small sofa and began to write my negative thoughts. It was my lowest point in nearly twenty-four years.

I wrote my perceptions about the months spent with an adult child back in the nest. Then, I wrote my feelings about caregiving: "I can't do this anymore. I thought I had it all together, but I don't." A few months earlier I had written down Scripture references that show caregiving is not a cross to be borne but a calling from the Lord. I sought encouragement by re-reading some of those verses. Then, I wrote, "Caregiving a calling not a cross? Bullshit!"

One truly honest statement broke the dam. A flood of emotions followed. "I'm feeling tired, discouraged, anxious. I have sudden nervousness and heart flutters for no reason or over *little* everyday things. I'm feeling confused. I go about simple tasks inefficiently, unfocused, with wasted motions and time. I'm feeling sad, lonely, cut off from the world, the kids (especially Amy), from life, from my husband. I'm short-tempered and impatient. I feel guilty about my temper and impatience." Such statements are classic symptoms of anxiety and depression. Yet, it was to be more than a year before I sought help.

A caregiver friend had given me a lovely little inspirational book written by a man who cared for his Alzheimer's stricken wife. I read it, hoping it would lift my spirits. It did not. Cynically, I wondered, "Does this author really *enjoy* caregiving that much? Is he really tender and loving *all the time*, or is he leaving something out?"

My own relationship with Ralph was a mess and I knew it. My caregiving had become perfunctory again. I could do the whole routine without ever looking him in the face, and often fed him entire meals in silence. On my pad, I wrote, "I can't take care of him anymore, and I can't let him go with our relationship, our love in a shambles. I feel we were robbed of the best years of marriage. *I* was robbed, cheated. Sure, 24 years are a drop in the bucket of eternity, but I mourn them, now. How do I get back or create a new loving relationship with Ralph?"

As soon as I wrote the question, I knew the solution. It was that Holy Spirit speaking thing, again. "The answer," I wrote, "probably is to get back a loving relationship with Jesus. It has been choked by the thorns of life (see The Parable of the Sower in Matthew 13) since last May." I listed some "thorns"—worries over Amy, Mom, finances, our lack of help, my health—and reiterated the feelings of hurt, grief, and overwhelming responsibility. Finally, I wrote this prayer: "Oh Jesus, love me; love through me; clear my mind and my time to be *with* you and *with* Ralph. Please. Amen."

My two-hour mini-retreat ended, and I went back to the old grind, which included 20-25 hours each week of unfilled attendant care time. The only difference was that I could call it a grind. I did not have to pretend anymore. I could acknowledge the emptiness inside me. I continued to feel parched and dry in spirit all through the rest of that winter, spring, and summer.

I did make more effort to communicate with Ralph, though. He was not interested in using his Eyegaze System and seemed to be having difficulty with it. So, I went back to our pre-Eyegaze technique. To discern his thoughts on issues of the heart, I talked to him, read to him, and asked for his reactions, positive or negative. When I didn't take time to initiate communication that way, we both suffered. One incident that summer illustrates.

Around midnight, I gave Ralph his sleeping capsule and pain pill and positioned him on his side as usual. By the time I got into bed, it was nearly 1:00 AM and I slept soundly—too soundly. I vaguely remember hearing Ralph moan, but without waking, I reached over and turned down the volume on the monitor. Over the noise of the air conditioners, I could not hear his panicked panting, a sound that usually alerted me to real trouble. When I finally did hear him moaning around 4:00 AM, there was an alarming note in his voice.

I found him totally rigid and tomato red. I didn't need to take his temperature to know it was sky high. Probably his blood pressure was, too. His medications had prevented him from sweating, and the situation was potentially dangerous. I stripped the covers off and struggled to sit him up. His left knee would not bend at all. After I poured two glasses of ice water into him, he relaxed a bit, but his heart rate and breathing were still too fast. When he finally went to sleep, it was nearly 5:00 AM. Then, I could doze again.

Around 10:00, I began trying to wake him to get more fluids and some food into him. It took until mid-afternoon for him to get reasonably awake and catch up on fluids. It took the rest of the week for the painful inflammation in his left knee to go down.

After the physical symptoms of that scary night had abated, Ralph seemed more distant, uninterested, and lethargic. He avoided eye contact and dozed through my attempted conversations. Four days later, I finally asked the question I had been afraid to pose. "Are you, or were you, angry with me for not coming to help you that night you were in so much pain?" He squeezed my hand for "yes."

I said, "I don't blame you. I am angry with myself. Can you forgive me?" He smiled just a little and squeezed again for, "yes," without any hesitation.

Since he responded so quickly, I asked, "Had you already decided to forgive me a couple of days ago?" He squeezed again.

"Then I could have saved myself a lot of guilt if I had asked you sooner." Ralph smiled again and let out a short chuckle. I said, "I love you," and kissed him. Our relationship was beginning to come together again.

Skip ahead to August 28. With drought evident inside and out, I went to the ear/nose/throat specialist for a check-up. Once more, he said he could see no physical reason for my sinus congestion and headaches. He wrote out the usual prescriptions for two nasal sprays and a pill. On the way to my van in the parking lot, I said aloud, "Lord, I am so tired of taking medicines." I was beginning to suspect that the sprays might be part of the problem. "I want to trust you to deliver me from them. Please, help me." I by-passed the drug store and drove on home.

August 31 was a rare Saturday when Florence volunteered to work, giving me a day of "Sabbath" rest. Alone in my office retreat, I picked up a favorite devotional book, *My Utmost for His Highest*, by Scottish missionary and evangelist Oswald Chambers. I turned to the entry for August 30 and read, "Keep your relationship right with [Jesus Christ], then whatever circumstances you are in, and whoever you meet day by day, He is pouring rivers of living water through you."[5]

The living water analogy is one Jesus used when talking to the Samaritan woman at the well. "Everyone who drinks this water (the well water) will be thirsty again, but whoever drinks the water I give him (spiritual water) will never thirst. Indeed, the water I give him will become in him a spring of water welling up to eternal life" (John 4:13-14). Such a spring of living water, Chambers notes, flows out to other people and waters their spirits without any effort on our part. He says, "It is the work that God does through us that counts, not what we do for Him."[6]

---

[5] Oswald Chambers, *My Utmost for His Highest*, (New York, Dodd, Mead and Company, 1935), 243.

[6] Chambers, *My Utmost for His Highest*, 243.

In the margin, I had made a note two years earlier to read the page to Ralph for his encouragement. He can do nothing, but he silently holds God's living water for those around him to drink. In 2002, I was the one who needed its message. As thirsty as I was, I could do nothing to encourage Ralph or anyone else. All I could do was stay close to Jesus, seek joy in him, pray for others, and be a vessel (pitcher, bowl, or hose) from which living water is free to flow.

On my notepad I wrote, "I am weary. I have been waking through the night and early morning, listening to the voices of worldly care and anxiety, which drown out the voice of the Lord. This is the first morning in weeks when I have had quiet time to be alone with the Word. How do I hear the Lord's voice on the busy mornings as well? Lord, please give me rest and help me hear your voice only."

Turning the page in *My Utmost for His Highest*, I read the devotional for August 31. Chambers comments, "The cares of this world, said Jesus, will choke God's word." (How true this had been for me!) In the next paragraph, he reiterates the idea from the previous page. "Be rightly related to God, find your joy there, and out of you will flow rivers of living water."[7]

---

[7]Chambers, *My Utmost for His Highest*, 244.

We had always come to a similar conclusion in our Tuesday Group: *nothing is as important as our relationship with God.* What joy we experienced as we praised him in prayer and song! How the living water sustained us between meetings! Saturday morning, August 31, 2002, searching for the joy I once knew in the Lord, the words of Scripture from John 4 touched my heart. A tiny trickle of living water bubbled up into my empty vessel. It would be enough to get me through the desert I had yet to cross.

At the bottom of the page, I wrote this footnote: "This is day four with no prescription nasal sprays and day three with no pills. The sinus headache finally began to go away last evening. Morning stuffiness has been clearing with only a saline spray. Thank you, Jesus! Please continue to help me and sustain me."

SChapter 19 Out of the Drought, Into the Desert

Watered by the Spirit, I made plans to visit Jenny and her family in their new home at West Point where Captain Steve was now a professor. Meanwhile, Ralph needed a little extra attention. He had been somewhat neglected over the summer while I dealt with the drought, literal and spiritual, and took Mom to chemotherapy appointments.

In September, Florence and I took Ralph on a weekend retreat for persons with disabilities. Then I took him to the dentist. Later in the month, we saw a surgeon about the possibility of straightening Ralph's cramped left hand. After the consult, Ralph indicated that the uncertain benefits were not worth the likely problems; he did not want to pursue the surgery. "I agree," I said to him. "Besides, that surgeon didn't even treat you like a person." Next day, I requested referrals for another round of nerve block injections.

Between calls to doctors, I began talking with the Eyegaze people about trading Ralph's computer for a newer model. He had not been able to use it for months. The problem, I learned, was age-related changes in his eye. His old system was not sensitive enough to compensate.

Mom's visit to the oncologist in early September did not go well. The lump on her forehead seemed to be growing again. Dr. C. stopped the chemo, ordered a new round of scans, and referred her to a radiation oncologist. Suddenly the calendar was more crowded that ever with appointments for Mom as well as for Ralph, along with reminders to call for and pick up the necessary referrals or films before each doctor visit.

In October, Mom underwent two weeks of daily radiation therapy. After the treatments were finished, Carolyn and Uncle John came for lunch on Mom's birthday, October 24. Amy joined us for the day, and we surprised Mom by adding a visit from my brother Bob and his wife Mary, their second trip across the state since Bob's heart surgery. Everyone's unspoken sense was that this might be Mom's last birthday. The menu included her special request—fried chicken livers. It was a low-key, poignant celebration.

The next morning, Florence moved in to stay with Ralph for the weekend, and I left for West Point. I need this mini-vacation, I told myself. September and October were rough. November promised to be easier. I hoped to do some writing and get ready for the holidays. When I got back from my trip, Mom and I planned a day to go shopping at a mall. It would be a nice change, since all of our recent outings had been to medical appointments. The Lord had other plans for us.

The morning of our shopping trip, Mom called. Her voice sounded strained as she said; "I can't go shopping. I twisted my foot." Instead, we visited in her cluttered studio apartment and "shopped" through catalogs. She was sitting in a wheelchair with the badly swollen foot wrapped in an ace bandage. X-rays that afternoon showed broken metatarsal bones, but it was several days before the swelling went down enough to cast the foot.

Mom did not deal well with this new disability. She expected a "walking cast" to allow her freedom, but the cast cut into her shin and made simple transfers excruciating. When the director of nursing told her they would have to move her into the nursing center, she was mad. She'd have been hopping mad if she could have hopped.

I knew the move was best. To make it a little more palatable for her, I arranged a consolation prize. The nurses agreed to take her to one of the TV lounges that evening so she could watch the Thursday night Pitt vs. Miami football game. This frail, hunch-backed, white-haired, 87-year-old lady was a diehard University of Pittsburgh football fan. Pain might deter her from taking care of her own physical wellbeing, but it would not stanch her school spirit.

After that, I went to see Mom at least four days a week. I took her to the oncologist in her wheelchair in our van. I wheeled her down the hall to her studio, so she could watch TV or use the phone. I made her start throwing out junk and sorting her piles of papers. She consented reluctantly, because I told her she couldn't come "home" until we rearranged her furniture so she could reach the call button from the bed. And we couldn't move furniture until we got the junk out of the way. She caught a cold, and after the stuffy nose cleared, she had a lingering cough. That made another reason to get rid of the junk; it was covered with eight years' worth of accumulated, lung-clogging dust.

December days, when I wasn't with Mom, I was often doing business for her. There were legal matters to be taken care of— things our lawyer had suggested she do after Dad's death six years earlier. Now that she was in nursing care, those transactions were imperative. I spent many hours with the business manager at the home and with the lawyer and on the phone and at the bank.

Again, Ralph got the short end of the deal. We had little quality time together, since I was preoccupied with Mom's needs. He did get his new Eyegaze Communication System, though, on November 20. With a more sensitive camera, faster processor, and improved software, it worked like a charm. Ralph quickly mastered "Score Four" and crushed all challengers. Of course, that made him laugh. It's hard to use an Eyegaze System when your eyes squint with laughter.

How was I holding up? I was definitely in a desert. I had less time than ever to spend in God's Word. Yet, I was not thirsty. I could see God's hand in the details of our lives: the caring of the nursing staff for Mom; the blessing of Ralph's new computer; the filling of financial needs; health and strength for each day. As I attempted to share comforting Scripture with Mom, the same passages reassured me. I started working on a Christmas letter to long-time, long-distance friends, telling for the first time ever, how Jesus makes a difference in our lives. In fact, the Spirit was compelling me to write with an urgency I had never felt before. Someone needed that letter—someone who could not wait for me to finish this book. Maybe it was Mom.

Mom got her cast off and moved back to her studio two days before Christmas. She was not ready to take care of herself, and we still had lots more junk to sort. However, an intestinal virus raging through the home necessitated giving her nursing center bed to someone sicker. The secretary called to say they were advising families not to come for Christmas; the entire building was under quarantine.

Two days *after* Christmas, with the flu epidemic waning, we went to visit Mom—Amy, Jenny, Steve, Ashley, Katie, Ralph and I. Mom's cough seemed worse. She fumbled weakly with the wrappings on her gift. While the rest of us watched, uncertain how to help, three-year-old Katie took charge of the situation. She popped up beside Mom and said, "I'll help you, Great-grandma. Here's how you do it." With that, she gave a vigorous rip to the paper. Great-grandma chuckled and coughed.

Chapter 20 The Straw that Broke the Camel's Back

From the Unks family, the big Christmas-time news was the engagement of our niece, Debra, to Brent, her "man of my dreams." Both of them were teachers at the Cairo American College in Egypt, where they had met. Jenny, Amy, and I speculated where the wedding would take place. Would they marry in Pittsburgh where Deb's parents, Ed and Kay, live? Or at Brent's parents' home in western Canada? Or somewhere else? I bet on somewhere else. Knowing Debbie, I pictured her getting married in Egypt in the shadow of a pyramid, then riding off on a camel to a honeymoon oasis. I was pretty close.

The invitation arrived by email January 15. The wedding would be Good Friday, April 18, 2003 in Egypt. Debbie wrote that she really hoped I could come and wanted to give me plenty of time to plan. For a brief few hours, I actually entertained fantasies about going. I talked with Jenny by phone. She had already checked airline ticket prices on-line. Reason prevailed, however. There were plenty of arguments against making the trip. Cost, for one, and Ralph's care while I would be gone. Besides, with war pending in Iraq, travelling to the Middle East seemed dangerous. I emailed my regrets to Debbie. As I clicked 'send,' I laughed and said, "Lord, if you want me to go to Egypt, you'll have to drop this one in my lap."

On my visits with Mom, I told her about Debbie's engagement, her wedding plans, the invitation, and my reply. Despite her own problems, Mom still seemed interested in what was going on with others. Maybe it was a diversion tactic. If she could keep me talking about something else, she put off working on the distasteful job of sorting through her piles of mail, magazines, and mementos. I knew she was not feeling well, though. One day, when I went into her room, she was sitting in her recliner as usual, but without the usual TV game show on. She was just sitting. When I asked, "How're ya doin'?" she replied, "I'm tired of hurting, tired of coughing, and tired of living."

A few days later, another email came from Debbie. I sat in front of the computer crying as I read, "Mum and I have discussed buying you a ticket to come over for the wedding. There isn't anyone, other than my parents and best friend, that I would rather be here. You are an inspiration to all of us as a person who has fulfilled her wedding vows through good and bad. I also can't think of anyone who deserves a vacation more than you, and I'd like to help provide that vacation."

After a few minutes, I took a deep breath, dried my tears and called Jenny. "Remind me," I said, "why we decided it would be irresponsible to travel to the Middle East at this time in history." I started to read her Debbie's email, but before I finished, she was screaming into the phone, "Mom, GO! I'll come and stay with Dad." Suddenly, I was out of practical excuses. I had to face my fear of travelling and choose. The Lord had dropped Egypt into my lap. Would I trust him to work out the details?

For three days, I wrestled with indecision. I sought Ralph's opinion. He said to go. I made mental note of all the preparation I would have to do—basic things like get a passport and a bigger suitcase, not to mention write a volume of instructions for Ralph's care. I told Mom about Debbie's offer. "If I go," I asked, "do you think you could hold on 'til I get back?" Mom answered, "Guess I'll have to." It was her way of giving me tacit permission. I emailed my acceptance to Debbie.

In February, I mailed my Christmas letter to old friends—earlier than usual. It was not an ordinary superficial listing of the year's accomplishments. It acknowledged the pain and heartaches of the past 25 years. It included excerpts from the testimony we gave at New Life church. It listed our reasons for celebrating our marriage and God's gift of faith in Jesus, for "*only* Jesus can give life purpose, meaning, hope, and joy."

Mom was one of the first people to whom I gave the letter. Her comment, next time I saw her: "That was a very nice letter." She was a woman of few words, but she collected words—words that touched her heart. That was why cleaning her studio was so difficult. She saved letters and cards, books, poetry, devotionals, and every church bulletin and newsletter she received. She hated to let any of them go. The sorting proceeded slowly. Her coughing grew worse. The doctor tried several medications, but none seemed to help.

Meanwhile, I applied for a passport and began to list things I would need to take on an international trip. Kay, my "travel agent," emailed possible flight schedules, and we discussed them by phone. She said she would hold off ordering the tickets so she could coordinate my arrival and departure times with Debbie's childhood friend who was to be the maid of honor.

February 24, I took Mom to the oncologist. Concerned about her cough, he ordered a new CAT scan of the chest. March 6, we went back to Dr. C. for the results. In his office, he posted the films on a lighted panel for us. The small lung lesion that had appeared in two previous scans did not seem to have grown. I had to step close to see the real problem—both lungs were filled with tiny white dots of tumor connected by a spider web of filaments.

To Mom, x-ray pictures and medical jargon were a mystery. Usually I had to translate for her. This time, I watched her carefully to see if she understood what Dr. C. explained in his soft voice. She remained stone-faced. We rode home in silence. Back in Mom's room, I helped her to her recliner and sat on the bed beside her.

"So?" she asked.

I swallowed hard and began, "The CAT scan showed tiny little tumors all over both lungs. That's the reason for your cough. Dr. C gave you a prescription for a much stronger cough medicine that should help."

"I don't want any more tests or chemo."

"I know," I said. "He is not recommending any." Tears came into Mom's eyes. "Are you afraid of dying?" I asked, gently.

Mom shook her head. After another minute, she dabbed her face with the crumpled tissue she always carried in one hand. "Well, let's get on with it," she said.

I knew that she meant, 'let's get on with the dying.' I let silence hang for a moment before I said, "At least you know where you're going and who your Savior is."

She nodded and smiled ever so slightly. Then another coughing fit took over.

After I left Mom in her room, I went to see the director of nursing. She began arrangements for hospice care, and we discussed how that would be coordinated with the residence staff. On my way home, I decided to call Kay that evening and tell her not to book a flight for me. When I walked in the door, a large, important-looking, overnight letter was waiting. Inside were plane tickets to Cairo.

My hands holding the non-refundable $1,000 tickets began to shake. My heart began to race. My stomach tied itself in a great big knot. My eyes began to leak. "This is the last straw," I thought. "I can't go to Egypt. I need to be here when Mom dies. I don't know when that will be. How can I plan a trip?" I did not sleep at all that night. Or the next night. Or the next. Mental pictures of the ensuing days flash through my memory in kaleidoscopic lights and darks—tender moments contrasting with anguish.

Chapter 21 Pillar of Cloud, Pillar of Fire

At last, I called our doctor for an appointment for myself. "What's the problem?" the receptionist asked. "Racing heart beat," I said. She worked me into the next morning's schedule.

After making my appointment, I met with a hospice nurse. She reassured me that medications could control Mom's coughing and keep her comfortable. Amy went with me for moral support. I needed her company and was thankful our relationship was growing closer, again.

Sitting on the edge of an examining table the next morning, I told my woes to our doctor. "I think you have a classic case of anxiety," he said, "but let's give you a thorough exam to make sure there are no physical problems." The nurse ran an EKG and drew blood. Dr. R. wrote two prescriptions. One was for a sedative to help me sleep at night, but not so soundly that I would not hear Ralph if he were in distress. The other drug was an anti-depressant used for treating anxiety on a more long-term basis. I should take it each morning and come back in a week.

With the help of the sedative, I slept that night for the first time in days. The anti-depressant, which I started the next morning, did not seem to do much except make my mouth dry and my stomach queasy.

On my visits with Mom, I read Scripture passages about heaven. I told her I loved her and would miss her.

Carolyn and Uncle John came to say their good-byes. We had lunch with Mom in the dining room at the home. She ate very little and could barely talk.

My feelings of depression deepened. I just did not care. I told Jenny I didn't want to go to Mom's funeral, which would be in Pittsburgh.

At 10:00 A.M. on Saturday, I found Mom sitting in her chair. Her bed had not been slept in, and she had not been given either her bedtime or morning cough medicine. The weekend aide and temp-agency nurse had overlooked her. "Why didn't you call for help?" I asked. "I just want to sit here and die," she said.

I helped Mom get to the bathroom. The exertion brought on a horrendous coughing spell. I could only watch and pray as she leaned on the sink spitting foam.

Jenny came to visit her Grandma. She brought pictures that Ashley and Katie had painted. Ashley's was a lovely, well-done, back-yard scene, but Katie's was the treasure—two smiling heads with legs and fluffy halos. She had told Jenny, "It's Great Grandma and me, because we both have curly hair."

Bob, Mary, and their daughter Beth came to say their good-byes. They brought pictures of their cats, since Mom loved cats, but she seemed to have trouble seeing them. They stayed with her the rest of the day, giving me a little break. Before I left, I asked the nurses to move her into the nursing center that evening. When I told Mom the plan, her face clouded with anger, and she gasped, "No! Not the shoebox." That was her name for the tiny room she had occupied in the nursing center with her broken foot. I said, "Mom, I asked them to. I don't want you to be forgotten again." Her expression softened somewhat.

Monday, Amy and I wheeled Mom to the weekly hymn sing in the nursing center. Mom said she wanted to go, but didn't try to sing, until Amy asked them to do one of Mom's favorite Christmas carols, "O Come All Ye Faithful." She sang it in Latin, "Adeste Fidelis."

I stopped the anti-depressant I was taking, because I could not stand the nausea and dry mouth side effects any more. Within a few hours, my mood began to improve. Dr. R. agreed that for me, the drug brought on depression. Since the sedative alone was helping, I should stick with that.

Wednesday afternoon, I took Mom to her studio so we could call her favorite nephew in Tennessee. It was another tearful good-bye.

The hymn-singing hospice chaplain gave Mom a personal concert. It included her favorite hymn, "Glorious Things of Thee Are Spoken," which happens to have the same tune as the Pitt Alma Mater.

I asked Mom what her favorite Scripture passage was. Her answer, after a moments' thought, was First Corinthians 13.

Again, I said good-bye to Mom. "You don't have to hang on 'til I get back from Egypt. You can go home to the Lord whenever you want."

On a Friday, I called the doctor for Ralph. He had been congested and coughing for three weeks and was getting worse instead of better. I did not feel well myself. I had caught the cough from Ralph and my ears were stuffy. Dr. R came to the house in the afternoon and prescribed antibiotics for both of us.

When I was well enough to go back to see Mom, I found she had been refusing her medications. I pleaded with her to take the cough and pain medicines that were offered. "Refusing them is not going to help you die any faster," I said. "It will just make you more miserable in the process." In a hoarse whisper, she replied, "Then I'll just be miserable."

Several people volunteered to stay with Ralph, while I spent extra time with Mom. I could see God's hand in arranging for them.

Again, I said my good-byes to Mom. In her tiny nursing center room, I gave her sips of water. I sat by her bedside holding her hand until my arm cramped from the awkward position. I kissed her good-bye and told her that I loved her, although she seemed to be sleeping soundly.

Sunday afternoon, April 6, as I was getting ready to go to the nursing home, I got the call: Mom was gone. I knew I had already said everything I needed to say, done everything I could do. It had been exactly one month since her final diagnosis.

God's perfect timing still amazes me. More amazing is the way he sustained my spirit during that month. Everything I read to Mom for her encouragement ministered to me as well. One time, I read from the retirement home's newsletter, in which their pastor quoted Jeremiah 17:7-8. "Blessed is the man who trusts in the Lord, whose confidence is in him. He will be like a tree planted by the water that sends out its roots by the stream. It does not fear when heat comes; its leaves are always green. It has no worries in a year of drought and never fails to bear fruit."

"Yes," I thought, "this describes how the Lord is sustaining me right now. I do trust you, Lord. I love you. Years ago, you planted me by the stream of your life giving Spirit. I am rooted in your Word, so that passages of comfort come to mind. You speak to me through reminders from others. The heat is on, now, but I do not need to fear."

I began to tell people that I knew the Lord would work out the details of Mom's passing and that he was helping me bear the stress, as well as providing for Ralph's care. I felt his presence with me. I talked to him constantly and asked him to guide my speech and actions. I was travelling through a desert of physical and emotional hardship, but it was very different from my spiritual drought, when the Lord seemed far away. This time he was going ahead of me every step of the way, just as he had led the Israelites through the desert of Sinai thousands of years ago.

"After leaving Succoth they camped at Etham on the edge of the desert. By day, the Lord went ahead of them in a pillar of cloud to guide them on their way and by night in a pillar of fire to give them light, so that they could travel by day or night. Neither the pillar of cloud by day nor the pillar of fire by night left its place in front of the people" (Exodus 13:20-22).

God planned the trip through Sinai for his children, the Israelites. He gave them food, water, and shelter along the way. Their clothes did not even wear out in those forty years (Deuteronomy 8:4). I am his child, and he has planned my trip, too. He goes before me to lead. I need only follow the obvious route he lays out for me. He takes care of the details. Can I trust him? Of course I can. The question is; will I trust him?

Following God through that desert, I longed for the ordeal to end, to reach the Promised Land. His Word assured me: "The Lord will guide you always; he will satisfy your needs in a sun-scorched land and will strengthen your frame" (Isaiah 58:11). When I was ready to give up, he said, "My grace is sufficient for you, for my power is made perfect in weakness" (2 Corinthians 12:9).

I began to see God's purpose in my trials. My drug-induced depression helped me understand other people's struggles with that disease better. I also learned that faith is no shield from stress, and there is no shame in seeking medical treatment. Singing praises to the Lord may lift my spirit for a while, but it cannot cure the physical effects of stress any more than it can cure a sinus infection. If I hear myself saying again, "I just don't care," I will know to seek help from a doctor as well as wise counsel from other Christians.

My desert journey compelled me to re-examine the question, why is there suffering? The Spirit led me to Peter's answer. "These [trials] have come so that your faith—of greater worth than gold, which perishes though refined by fire—may be proved genuine and may result in praise, glory and honor when Jesus Christ is revealed" (1 Peter 1:7).

Peter means that our faith and eternal wellbeing are far more valuable than temporary physical health and comfort. I have to face the truth; do I stay close to God when everything is going well? Not usually. I think *I* am in charge of my life then, and I am too busy enjoying the power trip to consider God. In bad times, I turn to God. That's when I find the deepest joy, knowing that Jesus has spared me from an eternity of the kind of grief and suffering I experience here on earth.

Chapter 22 Climbing the Mountain of the Lord

On Thursday, April 10, Jenny, Steve, Amy and I drove to Pittsburgh for Mom's funeral. We stayed at Ed and Kay's house. (They were already in Egypt for Debbie's wedding.) The service Friday morning was small and informal. Bob and I spoke about our memories of Mom. I read Mom's favorite Scripture passage from the Bible she had used to plan lessons for her sixth-grade Sunday school classes. We tramped through the cemetery in a steady drizzle to see the gravesite and left immediately afterward to drive back to Philadelphia.

Saturday and Sunday were a blur of last minute preparations and packing for Egypt. Monday afternoon, Jenny dropped me at Philadelphia International Airport. We had time for only a hurried goodbye at the curb before security waved her away. I stepped through the giant revolving door dragging my new, wheeled bag with piggyback carry-on strapped to it. *Can this really be me beginning the adventure of a lifetime?*

As we winged eastward across the Atlantic, the sun set behind the plane. Dawn broke in front four hours later as we crossed England on the way to Rome. I did not sleep. The jet engine roar was too loud in my ears, which were still stuffy from the infection three weeks earlier. Besides, I didn't want to miss anything. I would close my eyes and open them again a few minutes later to see if the North Star was still there. *How beautiful are your heavens from way up here, Lord!*

My connection in Rome went smoothly, but the flight to Cairo was rough, with a very shaky takeoff. It could have been frightening, if I were not confident that God had arranged this trip and was holding up the plane. On that flight, I had my first taste of being a foreigner. Conversations around me were unintelligible. Announcements were given in Italian, then Arabic, and last in English. Descending through the clouds over the Mediterranean toward a bumpy landing, I saw that Egypt is tan in color.

An expediter that Debbie had hired met me in the airport and zipped me through customs and baggage claim. Kay, Ed and our taxi driver, Mohammed (half the men in Egypt are named Mohammed), were waiting outside the gate. My next ride was more adventurous than the flight. If you think a cab in New York

City is wild, it's a kiddy-car compared to a Cairo cab. And that tan color I saw from the air is fine, sandy dust, which covers everything.

Debbie had planned a full itinerary—no time to recover from jet lag. The next morning I was rousted out of bed at 7:00 AM to go on another wild ride; this time it was camels at the Pyramids of Giza. Debbie snapped a picture of me on a camel named Moses with a pyramid in the background. In it, I'm gripping the saddle tightly and smiling through clenched teeth. By the time we mounted for the return trip, I had relaxed enough to let go of the saddle with both hands and take a few pictures myself.

We had 2½ days of sightseeing around Cairo and dinner parties with Debbie's and Brent's fellow teachers. We climbed up into the Great Pyramid, walked around the Sphinx, and explored the museum containing King Tut's gold. A friend of Debbie's guided our tour of Coptic Cairo, the oldest sector of the city. There, according to tradition, Pharaoh's daughter pulled baby Moses from the Nile River. It is also said that Mary, Joseph, and baby Jesus stayed there when they fled from King Herod.

In our travels, I could not help noticing how inaccessible Egypt is to the disabled. There are no curb cuts or ramps. Sidewalks are rough cobblestones. Concrete pavements are deteriorating and uneven. Debbie's third floor apartment was spacious enough for a wheelchair. However, the elevator barely held three adults standing, and we had to squeeze through its narrow door sideways. In all of Cairo, we saw only two people in wheelchairs, one blind beggar, and a handful of elderly pedestrians with canes. I asked several people, "Where are the handicapped?" I never got an answer.

The wedding was Friday on a sandy slope overlooking the Pyramids of Giza. One hundred guests in casual attire sat on oriental carpets for the ceremony. Urns of flowers marked an aisle. A carpeted path led to an elegant tent at the top of the hill where formal table settings and an elaborate buffet awaited. Debbie, in a simple blue linen dress, and Brent, in linen pants and shirt, exchanged their vows as the sun set. During the reception after dark, we had a panoramic view of the pyramids, lighted by colored floodlights with the twinkling lights of Cairo in the background. Spectacular!

The next day, the newlyweds took Mom, Dad, and Aunt Nancy with them for the honeymoon. The five of us headed east in an American-made SUV—by far, the most comfortable conveyance I had ridden since deplaning. We went through the Ahmed Hamdi Tunnel under the Suez Canal and out across the Sinai Peninsula. Following a flat ribbon of asphalt across the bare expanse of dirty sand, I thought of the Israelites crossing this same desert on foot thousands of years earlier. They met no one on their trek. Today, military outposts dot the region, and travelers must stop at each one. A few kilometers from the Israeli border, we made a sharp right turn at one of those checkpoints and headed south toward the resort town of Dahab on the Gulf of Aqaba.

The southern Sinai desert is mountainous and rugged. Here the road twists and turns as the elevation rises. Occasionally we saw a Bedouin tent against distant rocks, or passed a turbaned man with a camel, or veiled women tending goats. Other than these, there were no signs of civilization. I wondered, what do they eat, and where do they get water? After darkness fell, we saw no other cars or lights until we approached the seashore resorts. In stark contrast with the surrounding countryside, our brightly lighted hotel boasted palm trees, lawns, gardens and fountains. We were greeted like visiting royalty.

A day of rest at the resort revived these weary travelers for big adventure—climbing Mount Sinai. After breakfast the next morning, we drove inland past amazing rock formations. At a checkpoint, we turned onto a side road to the Monastery of Saint Katherine at the base of Mount Sinai. A small monument along this road marks the spot where the Israelites erected the golden calf while Moses was up on the mountain. Inside the monastery, we peeked into a small chapel built over the roots of the burning bush where Moses first talked with God. It was late morning by the time we started walking the winding, rock-strewn trail that ascends the mountain. "This isn't too hard," I thought, but by the time we got to the first rest stop I was lagging behind.

Rest stops on the Sinai trail are simple rock, wood and canvas structures. There, Bedouins in traditional garb greeted us, anxious to sell us bottled water or snacks. (We had brought our own.) Small bamboo huts next to the "store" were outhouses. Those were free, but tipping the proprietor seemed to be expected. Brent and Ed carried wads of paper Egyptian pounds for the purpose. (An Egyptian pound was worth about 17 cents American.) When we moved on, Coach Brent dropped back to give me tips on energy-saving hiking techniques.

By the second rest stop, I was winded. "I don't think I can do this," I panted.

Debbie assured me, "We don't have to go all the way to the top."

"But I want to go to the top," I said.

Brent flagged a passing Bedouin with camel, who was on his way down the mountain. They exchanged a few words in a mixture of Arabic and English, and Brent handed the man a twenty-pound note. Brent motioned me to come as the camel master commanded his animal to kneel.

Sinai camels are much smaller than the Saharan variety we had ridden to the Pyramids. This spindly-legged one reluctantly knelt on the sharp rocks of the trail so I could mount. I was still squirming to get comfortable in the lumpy, homemade saddle when the little camel suddenly lurched to his feet. Gripping the saddle horn, I leaned back sharply, and barely managed to stay on. The Bedouin guide tossed the lead rope over the camel's neck and said something in Arabic. At that, the camel began walking up the trail by himself. Everyone else was several paces behind us.

In the months of wandering my personal desert, I thought I had learned all I needed to know about trusting the Lord. This was a new kind of test. I looked down to my right and saw a sheer drop only inches from the feet of my steed. I sucked in my breath and instinctively leaned to the left. On the left, *if* I could have pried a hand loose from the saddle, I could almost touch the vertical rock wall of the mountain. And nobody was guiding this beast! "Oh, help!" I whispered.

The trail grew steeper. The little camel plodded upward. He held his head high in characteristic camel fashion, so he could not see his feet, yet they seemed to find the smoothest path among the rocks. Soon I noticed that the path was actually very well marked—by piles of green camel droppings. My trusty steed knew exactly where he was going. He climbed this trail every day. I might as well enjoy the scenery. *Did they pad this saddle with rocks?*

Life is a little like climbing the mountain of the Lord. We want to get to the top, but the way is hard, narrow, and treacherous. At times we have to rely on God's grace to carry us, and the ride may not be comfortable. Others have gone before us, experienced similar problems, cleared some boulders from the trail, and left behind their sufferings to show the way. "The smoothest path through life," I philosophized, "is marked by dung."

We all made it to the top of Mt. Sinai, climbing the last 700 stone steps on foot. At the summit, the panoramic view was as barren as the path we had ascended—a desert plane to the east and rugged rock mountains to the west. The sky was deep blue and the wind chilling, its bite moderated by warm sunshine, except in the shadows of the man-made structures, a church and a mosque. Many find reaching the top of Mt. Sinai to be a spiritual experience. I can't say that I felt any closer to God there than I did when he sustained me on the climb, or than I do every day in the valleys of life.

Two days later, as my return flight nosed into its final descent to Philadelphia International Airport, I pointed out landmarks to my French seatmate. "There's the Jersey shore. The dark green area is called the Pine Barrens. That ribbon of gray on the horizon is the Delaware River, and the airport is just beyond it." It felt good to be coming home.

I found much to appreciate. The color green for one: emerald green lawns and tree-covered hillsides shrouded in the yellow-green mist of new spring growth. Highway safety for another:

traffic lights at intersections, and motorists who heed them and stay within lane markings. The jonquils and bleeding heart that greeted me in my own yard. A husband who loves me. His dedicated caregivers. My bed.

By the time I walked in the back door, I had been on the road for more than 40 hours, starting with the seven-hour car ride from Dahab back to Cairo. We made a whirlwind auto tour of everything in Cairo that I had not yet seen, went shopping at the Khan El Khalili market, and had dinner in an Egyptian restaurant. I was an automaton by the time Debbie dropped me at the airport for my 1:00 A.M. flight to Paris. Another twenty-four hours in planes and airport lounges completed my transformation to Zombie. I barely greeted Ralph and Florence, glanced quickly through the pile of mail, took a shower and slept for twelve beautiful hours.

Resuming caregiving responsibilities the next day was like a vacation—so leisurely and restful compared to the pace of travel. The jet set life was fun, but it had its discomforts. Over the next few weeks, I shared my impressions and pictures with Ralph and friends, put together an album of my trip, reflected on the cultural differences, and prayed for the people I had met in Egypt. Sometimes at home, it had seemed like my caregiving work would never end. Remembering that beautiful trip reminded me that God's caring for me, in fact, never does.

As I settled into the routine at home, I had another job to do—the unfinished work of mourning Mom. While I had been away, my fresh sorrow had seemed like a distant memory. The day after I got back, I went to Mom's studio to begin cleaning it out. Standing in the middle of the room, I slowly looked around—same clutter, same dust, same incontinent smell, same bright April sunshine streaming through the tall windows. The TV was dark and silent. Mom would have reached for her clicker and turned it off the moment I came in, so she could hear all about my trip. But the recliner was empty. There was no one to tell my stories to. With a lump in my throat, I put some trash into a plastic bag and took it to the basement on my way out of the building.

It took almost two weeks to complete the task of removing Mom's stuff. Much of it came back to our house, where I spent spare moments over the next two months sorting cards, letters, pictures, books and programs. Through her correspondence with a handful of old friends, I got to know her a little better. She seemed to accept without regret the changes that age and failing health brought. How I wished she could tell me the stories behind many of her mementos. On the other hand, maybe untold tales of the past are not so important in light of heaven's impending glory. Hadn't she said, "Let's get on with it," when death was inevitable?

Mom's affairs were finally settled. Several boxes of papers and pictures were packed away in a closet awaiting the "someday" when I would compile them into a family history. Our calendar quickly became as full as ever, even without doctor appointments for Mom. But for a long time afterward, if the phone rang on a Sunday afternoon, I half expected to hear her voice on the other end "just checking to see how you're doing."

A few months later in 2003, I wrote the following: "My ongoing role of caregiver is comfortable. When I first brought Ralph home in 1979, it was my only option. Now, it is my choice. In the parable of the sheep and the goats (See Matthew 25:31-46), Jesus told the people who took care of others, 'Whatever you did for one of the least of these brothers of mine, you did for me.' When we serve another person as though serving Jesus himself, we are doing God's will and thus we are free. Ironically, the more we pursue our own ambitions and dreams, the more we are enslaved to ourselves and the world. I may appear bound by menial nursing chores, but when I do it for Jesus, I am free! It is freedom beyond earth-bound travel, a perspective higher than Sinai."

Chapter 23 Will You Marry Me?

The scene was the same whenever Jenny and her family arrived for a visit. Ashley and Katie were first in the back door, Ashley wearing her Mona Lisa smile, Katie talking a mile a minute. Jenny and Steve followed with one of them holding Thunder's leash, the other carrying the remnants of their snacks or take-out meal from the trip. We all crowded into the tiny hallway hugging, with Steve towering over the mass and Thunder nosing her way in at knee level.

So it was on Friday evening, December 19, 2003. The tree was decorated, the outdoor lights were up, the fudge was made, and I had just finished wrapping the presents. Despite my long-standing love/hate relationship with Christmas, I was looking forward to the busyness of the next four days.

After Katie and Ashley were tucked into their sleeping bags upstairs, the adults met in Ralph's room to go over the master plan. Saturday morning, we would go to the potter's supply store and get glazes for the pottery Jenny and the girls had made in the fall. Saturday afternoon and evening, Jenny and Steve were going to a wedding, so I would get to baby-sit *and* take care of Ralph. Sunday we would all rush home from church, grab a quick lunch and go to the premiere performance of Aunt Amy's new ballet company. We would give Amy Monday to recuperate and then have our family Christmas celebration on Tuesday.

Jenny stepped over to Ralph, who was sitting up in his hospital bed, and took his hand. "Looks like Monday will be the best day for our annual shopping trip, Dad. Do you want to do that?" He squeezed her hand for 'yes.'

"Do you have an idea what you want to get?" Ralph gave no squeeze, which means 'no.'

"Well, do you think you can narrow it down by Monday?" Ralph smiled a little and let out a short involuntary chuckle as he squeezed Jenny's hand again.

The weekend flew by at an exhausting pace. Monday, after an early lunch, I helped Jenny set Ralph up with his computer. He quickly ran through the eye tracking calibration and selected the typewriter program from the main menu. "You can go now, Mom," Jenny said. Obediently I left the room and closed the door. A short time later, Jenny opened it again, saying, "Okay, we're ready to go." As I gave Jenny a refresher course on strapping Ralph's wheelchair into the van, I dropped hints about sales on sweaters and warned, "Don't spend too much money; keep it simple and practical." Jenny and Steve drove off to the mall with my van and my husband.

The kids and I spent the afternoon baking cookies, drawing pictures, and checking on the progress of the kiln, which was firing their pottery in the basement. It was long after dark when the mall detail returned from their mission. While giving Ralph a drink, I watched curiously as Jenny slipped past on her way upstairs. The outline of a large cube-shaped box was evident through the plastic department store bag she carried. Definitely not a sweater. Hmmm?

Later, with Katie and Ashley again settled for the night, Jenny caught me alone in the kitchen. "Mom, I want you to know that the present Dad got you today was entirely his idea. He knew exactly what he wanted. He typed it out twice. With full sentences. I asked him some yes/no questions about details, but I couldn't make him change his mind." The hesitancy in her voice hinted that I might not like the gift.

"It can't be that bad, can it? Is it some kind of tool?" I made the guess based on the size and shape of the box. A few years earlier, I had asked for an electric drill, and Ralph and Jenny had had great fun shopping for it. This time, however, Jenny's tight-lipped expression told me I would get no clues.

"Just remember tomorrow—I had nothing to do with it. All I did was drive the van."

What kind of gift could possibly need such a disclaimer? Hmmm?

The atmosphere in the Unks household on December 23 was just like Christmas day, except that since it was not the actual holiday I had help with Ralph's morning care. Amy arrived for brunch, after which we all gathered in the living room for the ritual opening of the gifts. I sat on one end of the sofa with Ralph in his wheelchair beside me. In the pile under the tree, I spied the mysterious large cube, now disguised in burgundy paper. Of course, Jenny made sure to save it for later.

As soon as Ashley handed me the package, Ralph began to smile. (Remember that he could not do that on demand. He had no control at all over his facial expression. Smiles, chuckles, or laughter could only come from genuine feeling.) I opened one side of the paper enough to see the writing on the box and exclaimed with happy surprise, "A teakettle!" Ralph's smile grew bigger.

While removing the rest of the paper and opening the box, I went on talking to everyone in general. "I need a teakettle. I had to toss the old one a couple weeks ago, because the lining was flaking off." Then to Ralph, "Thank you! I didn't know you paid that much attention to what was going on in the kitchen. This is perfect. Practical. Not too expensive. Ya done good!" By now Ralph was actually laughing.

I was about to go put the teakettle on the stove when Katie exclaimed, "What about this one?" She pointed to a small package that I had not seen before among the few remaining under the tree. "You can give that one to Grammy," said Jenny, and Katie brought it over. To me, Jenny said, "That one is from Dad, too." Ralph was grinning.

Carefully I removed the ribbon and the paper. The suspense mounted. I opened a small, cardboard jewelry-type box. Twice before, Ralph had picked out a pendant necklace as an accessory to his gift. I hoped it wasn't another necklace. I don't wear jewelry much with my usual jeans. But I would be appreciative, anyway. Inside the cardboard box was a royal-blue velvet box. As I pulled it out, Jenny said, "Turn so Dad can see your face when you open it."

I turned toward Ralph, whose grin was growing. It took me a moment to figure out which side of the little velvet box would open. Then I slowly pulled back the spring-hinged lid.

Pause the DVD here and skip backward to a dark and sinister scene nine and one-half years earlier. I'm working for the church, and I rush off right after dinner to a vacation Bible school planning meeting. Ralph is at home with his attendant, a young man who has only worked for us for a couple of months. So far, he's been gentle and caring with Ralph, but he makes me uneasy. He's made inappropriate comments to our daughters and once came to work smelling of alcohol.

I come home from the meeting, and the attendant bolts out the door, probably to go drinking, I surmise. The kitchen has been cleaned up. Ralph is in bed. All is well. I stop to watch a little TV with Ralph before going to get ready for bed myself. Upstairs an hour later, I notice small things amiss. There is a crumpled paper towel on the bathroom floor, and my jewelry box is a few inches forward from its usual position on the dresser. I lift the lid. Everything seems to be there . . . except for a birthstone ring? I open the top dresser drawer. My good watch is there, so is my . . . Oh no! The box for my engagement ring is turned sideways. My heart skips a beat as I pick it up and open it. It is empty. I scream as if I have been stabbed and run downstairs crying to tell Ralph.

I feel violated. That attendant had no business being anywhere in the house except Ralph's room, the kitchen and the hallway between them. He went into my personal space and took the one thing in all the world most precious to me—precious not because of its monetary value, but because Ralph had given it to me as a token of his love and now could never replace it. Why, I lament, didn't he just take TV's or silverware.

Two years later, a police detective caught up with the young man in jail on an assault charge and learned he had sold my rings on the street that night for sixty dollars' worth of drugs. It took me a long time to get over the loss. In the process, my spirit had to do a lot of growing up with God's Spirit. You see, the most precious gift Ralph ever gave me was not a ring but himself. Through him, I came to know Jesus who gave his life so that I can live forever. Diamond ring? Eternal life? Which is more valuable? It's a no-brainer. I haven't even mentioned the loss of the ring in several years.

Fast forward back to Christmas 2003. Inside the little blue velvet box, tucked into its blue velvet lining, a single modest diamond sparkled on a thin gold band. I gasped softly. My eyes filling with tears, I looked at Ralph. If his grin could grow any bigger, it would surely split his face. I took the ring from the box and slipped it on. It was almost identical to the original one, a perfect match to the wedding band, and it fit, too. I grabbed Ralph's hand with both of mine and sat there crying silently.

Through a fog of tears, I could see Amy on the other side of Ralph dabbing her eyes. Behind me, I heard Jenny sniff. Steve, beside me on the couch, was very still and silent. Ashley and

Katie, on the floor among presents and wrappings, watched in wonder. Perhaps, the only one dry-eyed (besides Thunder) was Ralph. He just kept grinning. I felt as if he had asked me to marry him all over again, and of course, my answer was YES. "I love you," I whispered.

Chapter 24 Seizure

I don't know how the silence of that long, magical moment was finally broken, but the excited chatter afterward confirmed what I had begun to suspect. The teakettle was Jenny and Steve's suggestion—a ruse to keep me guessing about my real gift, the one Ralph wanted to buy. No wonder Ralph laughed when I praised his choice of a practical gift. The rest of the afternoon passed quickly with lots of mirth and an early Christmas dinner before Jenny's gang started their three-hour drive home to West Point. After giving Ralph his sleeping capsule, I fell into bed exhausted.

Christmas Eve morning, I woke up coughing. Florence came to get Ralph up, and I went back to bed. The rest of that day and the next drifted by in a feverish fog. Attendants came and went during the day. Amy came and stayed for three nights. The Lord gave me *his* strength to do what I needed to do. I got to the doctor the day after Christmas. He said I had the flu and it would take three to five days to run its course.

By then, Ralph was sounding congested, too, and that had me worried. As I began to feel a little better, he grew worse, coughing and wheezing. *Don't check out on me, now,* I thought. *We just got engaged all over again.* To Ralph, I simply said, "I love you," but I'm sure he saw the concern in my face.

New Year's Day, Maria, who was a nurse, was there. She listened to Ralph's chest and heard crackling on the lower right side when he was lying down. Sitting up he sounded fine, so I waited until the next day to call the doctor. January 2, the doctor's office was still operating with a skeleton holiday staff, and a nurse told me, "Take him to the emergency room." After twelve hours in ER with dozens of other coughing people, Ralph was finally admitted to the hospital and given a bed. Still weak and drained from my own bout with the flu, I went home to catch a few hours' sleep.

The next morning, I called Amy and Jenny, our pastor and the day's helpers, who would need to know not to come to the house.

During Ralph's five-day stay in the hospital, my daily routine felt weird: leaving the house in the morning, sitting around in the hospital all day, eating leftovers and returning phone messages before bed. During each day, several doctors, a nurse practitioner, respiratory therapists, and a speech therapist made their rounds. I kept a list of questions for each and found the waiting exhausting. However, we were encouraged by friends, old and new, who dropped in to visit or sent cards.

Between visits and consultations, I did some of Ralph's care—giving him a shave, changing his catheter, readjusting the pillows between and under his legs, feeding him. I showed nurses how to feed him and position him so he would be more comfortable. It was like training brand new attendants each time the shift changed. Thankfully, the nursing staff respected my experience, solicited my input, and carried out most of my suggestions. Apparently, they were all talking about the quadriplegic man with perfect skin and the woman who had cared for him for an amazing 25 years. As hospital stays go, this one was better than most.

By the second day, Ralph's initial diagnosis of pneumonia was modified to bronchitis with a possible hiatal hernia. Intravenous fluids, antibiotics, and breathing treatments alleviated the bronchitis. For the hernia, an internist prescribed antacids and a very strong laxative. Though Ralph's chest congestion improved, one troubling symptom persisted: he choked on drinks. A speech therapist evaluated his swallowing function and ordered a thickening powder for liquids to help them go down easier. With the consistency of pea soup or strained applesauce, each drink had to be spoon-fed—a very time-consuming way to give eight glasses a day.

The evening after Ralph's release, Marty called. She had heard about his hospitalization by the grapevine and apologized for not calling sooner. I apologized for not calling her myself with the news. We shared a blessed few minutes in prayer, thanking God for the good things that had happened during the week and for his power and presence throughout. I felt God's peace. Marty reinforced that as usual.

As the weekend approached, we anticipated going to church for the first time since before Christmas, despite a bitter cold weather forecast. One problem puzzled me. Whenever I put food or drink into Ralph's mouth, he would begin a low, involuntary moaning. He seemed to be straining to swallow anything, and frequently coughed or gagged. *What's going on, Lord? Is this the way it's going to be from now on?* A deep sense of concern and a vague uneasiness settled over me.

Saturday night, I put Ralph into bed and raised it to a sitting position so he could watch TV while I took my shower. After I dried my hair, I laid out Ralph's clothes, and set up his medications for the next day. Then, I gave him his bedtime pills with a little lemon pudding and a drink. It was just after midnight when I put down the spoon and reached for the TV remote sitting next to the clock radio on the dresser. I clicked off the TV and turned back to Ralph to lay him down for the night.

A strange, wild-eyed look had come over Ralph's face. He seemed to have stopped breathing. *Is he choking?* With my arm around his shoulders, I pulled him forward so any thickened juice that might still be in his mouth could spill out. Nothing did and he still didn't breathe. Suddenly, he gasped and began to shake violently. *A seizure! Stay calm. He's had one of these before. It'll pass in a minute or two.* I held him in my arms and told him, "It's okay. You'll be alright. Jesus is with us." The bright green numbers on the clock radio read 12:09.

Two scenes flashed through my memory. One was of Ralph's last seizure, probably 23 years before. His bed was in the dining room then. In the very early morning hours, I heard the side rails rattling as his trembling legs banged against them, and I ran downstairs. The crisis passed almost as soon as I got to his side. Afterward he slept soundly. I let him sleep and waited until a more reasonable hour to call the doctor. The visiting nurse came to check him over, and by evening, he was fine.

Scene two took place in our laundry room about fourteen years later. I was spooning cat food into a bowl when our pet cat began thrashing about on the floor. At first, I thought she was chasing a bug. When I realized she was in some kind of distress, I knelt beside her, stroking her long, soft fur and talking to her as she began to calm down. *She must have had a seizure.* I expected she would sleep for a while as Ralph had. I would move her to her favorite spot on the carpet in front of the heater vent. But she wasn't breathing! I lifted her limp head and felt her throat for a pulse. There was none.

12:11 A.M. Ralph's body was straight and rigid, extended across the peaks of the bed, which was still bent into a sitting position. Tremors shook his limbs. His breathing came in rapid gasps. His face was bright red; his eyes fixed on the ceiling in a glassy stare. With one arm, I held him, while my other hand reached for the bed control and fumbled for the right button to recline the head. *Oh Lord, help us.* The seizure continued without abatement. *What should I do? Should I call for help?* "You're okay. I love you. Everything's gonna be alright." The calmness in my own voice surprised me and mocked my racing heart.

12:15 A.M. *This should be stopping by now.* Ralph's strenuous gasping scared me. *Could he go into cardiac arrest? Or maybe have a stroke?* I looked at the phone on the other side of the room. *Too far away. I don't want to leave his side while I call.* I pulled my arm out from behind his head and *raced* to get the cordless. In seconds, I was back, pushing buttons 9-1-1 with the thumb of the hand holding the phone, stroking Ralph's twitching face and trembling arm with the other hand. "My husband is having a seizure," I said to the operator.

The world shifted into slow motion. I repeated the problem to the medical dispatcher, and gave the address three times while they tried to locate us on their maps. By the time the voice on the phone pronounced that paramedics were on the way, Ralph's tremors had finally begun to slow. 12:20 A.M. The seizure had lasted more than ten minutes. It was several more agonizing minutes before I saw flashing lights through the blinds and heard a diesel engine backing into the driveway. Ralph was still rigid and gasping.

The ER that night was practically empty, yet we waited. Waited for lab results on blood samples. Waited for a CAT scan of Ralph's brain. Waited for a radiologist to read the scan. Waited for a doctor to put it all together. Waited for a bed for admission. I sat beside Ralph watching him and watching the reflections of light in the diamond he had given me for Christmas. *Is this to be his final gift to me?* His muscles remained tense and spastic. With his mouth open, his tongue protruded slightly, doing a funny fluttering motion that I had never seen before. His eyes were sometimes open and staring, sometimes closed. He was unable to squeeze my hand.

His first hopeful response came around five o'clock in the morning when a new doctor entered and spoke to him—a lovely, young woman doctor. Ralph's eyes opened and drifted in her direction. *Hmmm, I'll have to tease him about that.* When I spoke, his eyes turned back toward me standing on the other side of him. Shortly after that, he was moved to a private room on the cardiac floor where he could be closely monitored. The gray light of dawn was beginning to show when I got home at 6:00. I tried to get a little sleep and made some phone calls before returning to the hospital.

Chapter 25 Family Meeting

Later Sunday evening I called Marty. "I wanted you to hear it from me this time," I said. "Ralph's back in the hospital." The whole story came spilling out concluding with, "Marty, he looks like he did after the original brain hemorrhage, when they were calling him semi-comatose."

"Oh, Nancy!" Marty didn't ask about the doctors' prognosis. We both knew it's God's plan that counts. "What's your gut feeling about this?" she asked.

"That it may be the beginning of the end." I said it with a catch in my throat. "But I have to tell you about our Christmas. There wasn't time the other night." By the end of my story of the teakettle and the ring, we were both in tears.

"That's such a beautiful love story!" Marty said. We prayed together, and she promised that she and John would see us at the hospital the next day.

Monday morning, I found Ralph much more relaxed and responsive. The speech therapist was working on feeding him when I got there. I watched her put small bits of applesauce into Ralph's mouth and try various techniques to stimulate swallowing. Each time, the applesauce dribbled back out. I tried my hand, pressing lightly on the middle of his tongue with the spoon—a trick that had always worked before. Still nothing happened. The therapist cleaned out his mouth with a swab so he would not choke on the leftovers and said she would try again later. Ralph followed the whole process with his eyes and smiled a little at our efforts.

By the time the doctors made their rounds late in the afternoon, they would have the speech pathologist's report indicating that Ralph could not swallow. I knew what their recommendation would be. A feeding tube was not new to us. Ralph had had one when he was comatose. The visiting nurse took it out at home, after we were sure he could drink enough liquids by mouth. My question for the doctors this time would be how soon we had to make the decision.

Meanwhile, we had a lot of rejoicing to do. Ralph was awake and alert, understanding and answering questions, and, best of all, smiling. A steady stream of visitors throughout the day shared our joy and praised the Lord with us. Jenny had come down from West Point for the day, leaving the kids at home with Steve. Amy

got a substitute for her afternoon classes. Marty and John were
there. Several other friends came and went at different times.

Marty wanted to see my ring, of course. I stretched my arm
across Ralph's bed between us so she could admire it, and we
giggled like schoolgirls. Ralph, watching us, began to smile. John
congratulated Ralph on his selection. Jenny told about their
shopping trip to buy the ring and about the strange looks they got
from sales people. Ralph grinned. "Did you explain the situation?"
I asked. "No," Jenny said, "It was more fun to keep them
guessing." Ralph chuckled. His tongue still did the funny flutter,
but he seemed to smile more easily than he had before the
seizure.

When other visitors had gone and only Jenny and Amy were
left, we talked briefly about the feeding tube decision. With my
hand in his, I posed the question to Ralph. "If your swallowing
reflex doesn't come back, do you think you want to have a feeding
tube that goes directly into your stomach? Squeeze if you do." I
felt no response. "Squeeze if you think you do *not* want the tube."
His fingers twitched weakly against my palm. "Are you getting
tired of life with disability?" Again, I felt a light squeeze.

Silence reigned in the room. I searched Ralph's face for a hint
of his deeper thoughts. He closed his eyes. It had been a long and
tiring day. I leaned over and kissed him on the forehead, saying, "I
love you." Amy wiped her eyes. After another moment, Jenny

said, "I want you to know, Dad, that I'll support whatever decision you make. It's up to you."

A short time later, the girls and I prepared to leave. Jenny had a long drive ahead of her. Amy needed to get back to her studio for her last evening class. With coats on, we took turns stepping up to Ralph's bed to say goodnight. "So. Dad," said Jenny, "next time you want to get us all together, just call a family meeting, okay? You don't need to have a seizure." Ralph laughed out loud.

Tuesday was a much quieter day. Ralph slept more, and his hand squeeze felt weaker. It was day three with no food, only intravenous glucose. The doctors had not pushed for a decision on the tube yet, but I felt we needed to make it soon, while Ralph still had the strength to give some input. Amy came to lend support. Jenny called to see how we were doing. She had me hold the phone to Ralph's ear while she told him again that she would go along with his decision. Our friend Debbie D. was the only other visitor.

Debbie had been coming about once a week to read to Ralph. She had lived with disability and pain for most of her forty-some years because of congenital hip deformities and scoliosis. She had helped give voice to Ralph's feelings about life with disability. I put Debbie on the spot by asking, "Have you ever felt you just wanted to give up?" Her answer was carefully thought out and faith full. She admitted to discouragement but never to the point of wanting to end her life. She trusted Jesus to help her bear the pain and take her home in his time.

A social worker had given us a blank living will form. I searched it looking for some help with our decision and read aloud the following: "I direct my physician to withhold life-sustaining treatment, *if* I should be in a terminal condition or in a state of permanent unconsciousness."

"You know," I said to Ralph, "You don't meet these conditions for being able to refuse a feeding tube. You don't have a terminal illness, and you're certainly not permanently unconscious." His eyes popped wide open. "That's something to think about." I listed some of the pros to life with a tube, such as not having to strain to eat or worry about choking, and being around to laugh at special family times. "It may be a lot of work, too, but if you're willing to go on living, I'm willing to go on taking care of you." There was a little twitch of a smile on Ralph's face. Amy was wiping tears again.

Later that afternoon, Ralph was taken to another part of the hospital for an EEG. Amy and Debbie left, and I sat alone in his room. Leaning back in a futile attempt to get comfortable in the straight-backed chair, I prayed for guidance, closed my eyes, and waited. The answer came with calm, reasoned assurance. For Ralph to refuse the feeding tube when he was not terminally ill would be slow suicide. But I was the one who would have to sign the permission or denial, since I had his Power of Attorney for health care decisions. For me to allow him to refuse the tube would be murder. I could not do that.

Okay, Lord, I hear you. Now I need some consensus. Amy had told me before she left that she was not ready to lose her Dad yet, so I felt she would agree. Then the phone rang. It was Jenny calling back. "I've been thinking," she said, "I'll still support Dad if he doesn't want the feeding tube, but I don't think he should get off that easy. Will you tell him that for me?" *Thank you, Lord.* Now the only person left to poll was Ralph.

After Ralph was settled into bed again and the afternoon nursing rounds were done, I moved my chair close, took his hand and said, "Okay, we have to talk. I know you get tired of struggling with this whole disability thing. I do, too. I look forward to the day when you'll be free and whole and we'll be together with Jesus in heaven. For now, we have a moral dilemma. Your body is healthy, even if it doesn't do everything you'd like it to do. To starve it to death would be suicide for you, murder for me. I can't do that to you. From what I hear, it's not a pretty way to go.

"We have lots of things to enjoy together, yet. There are people who need you to pray for them—Amy, Jenny, Steve, Ashley and Katie, lots of relatives, and me. Maybe your prayers have kept me going all these years. Lord knows you need me safe and healthy to take care of you."

I told him that Amy had said she wasn't ready to lose him yet. I told him about Jenny's second call of the day and her message for him. He smiled a little at that. I went over what the doctor had told us about how the tube would be inserted—without major surgery. Then I asked, "Are you willing to have the feeding tube and stay with us a while longer?"

Ralph's squeeze was not the most enthusiastic one he had ever given, but it was deliberate. "I'm glad," I said. "I'm not ready to lose you yet either." I paused, looking into his face as his eyes met mine. "I love you."

Chapter 26 A New Friend

The procedure for placing the tube in Ralph's stomach was done Friday afternoon. It took ten minutes with a little sedation and local anesthetic. Nurses began slow feedings that night and gradually increased them over the weekend. Monday they started giving medicines through the tube. A discharge coordinator arranged for delivery of the canned liquid food and new equipment we would need at home.

Tuesday was release day. The resident doctor and a nurse loaded us up with instructions, prescriptions, precautions, and enough food to hold Ralph until his supply arrived later that afternoon. I knew his care would be more work than before, but I had no idea how hard it would be.

Working out the details of the routine took two-and-a-half months. The attendants and I learned by trial and error together. Anti-seizure medicine had to be given at eight-hour intervals *not* near feedings. Other medicines had to be given *with* feedings. Feedings took about an hour each, after which Ralph's head had to be kept elevated for another hour or more; he could not be rolled for dressing or exercise with a stomach full of liquid.

Complicating matters were all the rashes Ralph had acquired in the hospital. Ten days there had ruined his "perfect skin." His primary care doctor made a house call to examine him and prescribed three different creams to fight a fungus infection, a bacterial rash, and a contact dermatitis. Keeping track of when and where to apply each cream needed detailed notes.

Regulating fluid input and output was a balancing act. We kept a written record. Ralph's discharge orders restricted water in addition to the liquid feedings, but that led to darkened urine and constipation. Another day in the emergency room failed to fix that problem, so I made up my own plan. I put him on a juice diet for two days—prune juice, cranberry juice, apple juice, broth and water. The urine cleared up and bowels began to move again. Then I reintroduced the feeding solution, continuing lots of extra water and juices. I made a chart showing times and amounts for feedings, medicines, and drinks, typed it on the computer, printed and posted it. Each time penciled changes accumulated, I revised and reprinted the schedule.

Sleep was in short supply. Six hours after getting his bedtime medicines, Ralph would begin waking. His bed creaked loudly as his legs stiffened, and he soon began to moan if I didn't get there to sit him up quickly. That meant I had about five-and-one-half hours to sleep. Remember when I said my idea of decadent luxury was eight hours of uninterrupted sleep? Well, with the new schedule, I would have settled for six. The afternoon *might* leave time for a twenty-minute nap, *some* days.

During the first five weeks, I went out only to go to the drug store or supermarket, except for one day in about the third week. I went to the mall, walked the length, and bought some underwear, then had a cup of wonton soup and an egg roll in the food court. Which world, I wondered as I sipped my soup and watched people, is the real one? This noisy, crowded lunch scene at the mall? Or the quiet, isolated daily care of a homebound patient? And how many of these carefree diners are future family caregivers?

The months following Ralph's seizure in January 2004 were stressful and sad. The demands on my energy seemed endless. Ralph's gag reflex improved a little, lessening the danger of his choking on his own saliva and mucous, but his ability to swallow did not return. It was hard to watch him suffering with "minor" annoyances like constipation, urinary infection, and leg cramps. I found myself asking, *Why, Lord, have you brought him through this crisis for more pain?* "How long, O Lord . . ." (See Psalm 6:2-4). In many ways, the emotional drain was similar to 1979, when Ralph first came home as a quadriplegic. There was one big difference, though—Jesus' tangible presence!

I wrote at the time, "I've been sad, but not devastated. I have been anxious but not in terror, stressed but not overcome. Paul describes the experience in his second letter to the Corinthians. 'We are hard pressed on every side, but not crushed; perplexed, but not in despair; persecuted, but not abandoned; struck down, but not destroyed. It is like carrying around the death of Jesus in our own body so that the life of Jesus may also be revealed in our body' (2 Corinthians 4:8-10). In other words, I wrote, the fact that we have strength to go on functioning is evidence of the power of Jesus' Holy Spirit in us."

While Ralph had been hospitalized, Marty reminded me of some encouraging Scripture verses we had shared many times before:

"Do not let your hearts be troubled. Trust in God; trust also in me" (Jesus speaking to his disciples in John 14:1).

"You will keep in perfect peace him whose mind is steadfast, because he trusts in you" (Isaiah 26:3).

Trusting brings peace of mind, but maintaining a steadfast attitude of trust requires focusing on God, not circumstances. Doing that does get a little easier with practice, although I'd prefer not to have more opportunities to rehearse my God-focusing and trusting skills. When I succeed, I find Christ's word is true: "My grace is sufficient for you, for my power is made perfect in weakness" (2 Corinthians 12:8).

Once we settled into a routine with the new medicines and tube feedings, we found there were a few advantages. For Ralph, he did not have to strain to swallow food or worry about choking on it. His face and throat muscles seemed more relaxed and he smiled more easily. For me, I did not have to spend much time cooking. I grilled my meats, ate my vegetables raw as salads, and stocked up on sandwich fixings and frozen entrees. That way I gained a little resting time.

Travel with Ralph was much harder. We made a day trip the summer of 2004 to meet Jenny and her family at her in-law's home in New Jersey. That September, with Florence's help we did an overnighter to West Point so Ralph could see the Academy before the family moved to Steve's next assignment. After that journey, we knew that longer, overnight stays would be impossible without a hospital bed. Our backs could not take working with him on a low bed, and Ralph could only sleep sitting up.

In the fall of 2004, a friend put a notice on the church email asking for volunteers to help us by giving Ralph his 11:30 P.M. medicines, so that I could go to bed a little earlier. A nearby night owl named Sylvia responded. She proved to be an angel, giving me at least an hour more sleep two nights a week. One afternoon, she came to spend a little time getting to know Ralph when he was more awake. We showed her his Eyegaze System and I explained how we had been searching for years for a programmer to adapt a chess game. She was intrigued and promised to talk to her computer-whiz nephew.

When Sylvia told her husband, John, about Ralph's interest in chess, John said, "Why can't I play with him the old fashioned way?" The next week, John came to try. We set up the chessboard on a small folding table and showed him how Ralph squeezes with his hand to indicate a yes response. John proceeded to point to possible moves. I walked away thinking it would take them an hour to make just one move. Apparently, when both players know the game, the choices are limited. By the second week, they had worked out their own system where Ralph kept his eyes on the board as John pointed to the moves, then made eye contact when John got to the one he wanted.

They began playing for an hour on Tuesday afternoons, and it was the highlight of Ralph's week. In a little over a year, they completed more than 30 games with wins and losses evenly divided. I could tell from another room when the game was going Ralph's way; he would laugh a sneaky sort of laugh because he couldn't do a poker face any more than he could force a smile. It was good to hear and see him enjoying himself. I think that's one reason God brought him through the seizure crisis. We thanked the Lord for Ralph's new friend, John.

Chapter 27 "He Will Quiet You with His Love"

Chess was a blessed distraction for Ralph throughout 2005, as he became increasingly plagued with pain. When lying flat, his limbs went rigid. He moaned loudly or started panting and grew red in the face. Bathing, dressing, and exercising became nightmares of torture for him and everyone who had to work with him. He had gained weight on the tube feedings. We cut the amounts, but he was still bloated and puffy, which increased his discomfort. The situation gradually worsened.

In the summer, Ralph's monthly blood work began to show gradual increases in his liver enzymes. At doctors' suggestions, we cut down on two of his medications, but enzyme levels continued to rise. By November, they were beyond the normal range, and his level of pain at an all-time high. Doctors only said 'wait and see.' Secretly I began to fear serious disease.

Saturday, December 17, as we were preparing to go to Amy's annual Christmas ballet, Ralph began vomiting his lunch. Needless to say, we missed the performance. When he still could not keep anything down the next morning, I called the doctor. Our weekend attendant helped get him up, and Ralph and I headed for the ER instead of church. Diagnosis: pancreatitis. Cause: the anti-seizure medicine he had been taking for nearly two years. Treatment: change the medicine and give intravenous fluids so the digestive tract could get a complete rest.

We spent five days in the hospital—six, if you count the day in the emergency room. Ralph came home December 23 with new medicines (actually fewer medicines) and a new kind of food. I came home with a new perspective on Christmas preparations: they don't really matter! We went to church Christmas Eve, just 24 hours out of the hospital. We had the tree trimmed by Ashley and Katie with a little help from Steve. Christmas day, we had chicken nuggets, pizza, family together time, and only one batch of fudge. Who needs more, really? The presents were cool, especially Ralph's. It was a really nice wooden chess set. I had ordered it just before he got sick and John picked it up for me while Ralph was in the hospital.

The new medicine schedule was simpler. As Ralph's pancreas healed, he lost the abdominal distention, bloating and edema. He was more relaxed when he had to be in a prone position for his care or exercise, and he was much easier to manage. He slept better at night, which meant I got a little more sleep. He was enjoying chess with John again on Tuesday afternoons.

We were able to see God's hand in bringing us through yet another crisis. I still couldn't spend eight hours in an emergency room singing like Paul and Silas in prison. But I could and did sense that God was with us and in control. I knew he loved us and was pleased with us. His presence, his love, calmed my secret fears, just as Ralph's embrace had quieted my sobbing years before on the night before his cerebral hemorrhage.

"The Lord your God is with you,

he is mighty to save.

He will take great delight in you,

he will quiet you with his love,

he will rejoice over you with singing" (Zephaniah 3:17).

Back in 1978, hope had kept us going. First, it was hope for Ralph's life. Then for healing. As we came to know Jesus, we looked forward to a Revelation 21 hope in heaven: "He [God] will wipe every tear from their eyes. There will be no more death or crying or pain, for the old order of things has passed away"

(Revelation 21:4). Gradually we found that the greatest blessings of God are already ours when we let go of our plans and dreams and depend on Jesus Christ. His peace and joy sustain us.

Joyous eternal life is not something we have to wait for until after we die. When Jesus prayed to his heavenly Father before his crucifixion, he said, "Now this is eternal life: that they may know you, the only true God and Jesus Christ, whom you have sent" (John 17:3). Eternal life begins as we get to know Jesus. That is something even Ralph could do. Ralph had a hell-on-earth of pain, an existence most people would consider neither death nor life. He looked forward to heaven knowing that Jesus spared him from an eternity of such grief and suffering. No wonder he agreed that he "would rather be in this wheelchair knowing Jesus than on my feet without him."

In 2005, I wrote, "I admire Ralph's tenacity, strength and endurance. I appreciate that he never complains, argues, or accuses. I am thankful that he made wise decisions years ago that continue to benefit us, and I respect his yes/no/caution opinions. I am humbled every time he spells out "ILOVENANCYVERYMUCH" on his computer. It takes great effort for him to do that. (That's why he shortcuts by skipping the spaces between words.) I celebrate my marriage to him, because it has led me to Jesus and saved me from hell. The example of Ralph's courage will help me get through whatever kind of suffering the Lord has planned for me in the future.

I also know that Ralph's courage and endurance do not come from within his personality any more than the strength to care for him exists within me. Even our faith is a gift from God. (See Ephesians 2:8-9) **This is not another triumph-of-the-human-spirit story. It is a triumph of the Holy Spirit."**

At their last meal together, Jesus told his disciples about his coming death and resurrection and promised to send them his Holy Spirit to guide and comfort them. He said, "I have told you these things, so that in me you may have peace. In this world, you will have trouble. But take heart! I have overcome the world" (John 16:33). Years after writing his Gospel, John wrote a letter to believers saying, "Who is it that overcomes the world? Only he who believes that Jesus is the Son of God" (1 John 5:5).

Having believed that Jesus is God's Son, we too received his Holy Spirit. He gave us peace, hope, joy, guidance and comfort even while we experienced the troubles of the world. That is a victory! Just look around at so many fearful, anxious, stressed, unhappy, angry, loveless, hopeless faces. Thank you, Jesus, for saving us from ourselves! How can we not love you, Lord?

"And we know that in all things God works for the good of those who love him, who have been called according to his purpose." (Romans 8:28) We were beginning to glimpse, in 2005, some of the eternal good coming from our years of life with disability, and were thankful that God had drawn us close to him. He had shown us countless examples of his faithful caring, so that "I am convinced that **neither death nor life**, neither angels nor demons, neither the present nor the future, nor any powers, neither height nor depth, nor anything else in all creation, **will be able to separate us from the love of God that is in Christ Jesus our Lord**" (Romans 8:38-39).

Chapter 28 Changing Scenes

Don't get the wrong idea from my upbeat account of our spiritual status. Life with disability is still drudgery. It's tedious, painful and exhausting for both the disabled person and the caregiver. A good day is simply boring. After the pancreatitis crisis, our routine of boredom, drudgery and tedium punctuated by bouts of pain and exhaustion lasted nine more years. God's grace carried us and there were times of joy. But, that didn't make daily life any easier. As the years became a kaleidoscopic blur, notable moments come into focus.

In a recurring scene, it is night. Ralph is in his bed sitting up to watch the late news. I am in the kitchen a few steps away, cleaning up, setting up meds for the next day, and preparing the bedtime medicines. He's moaning softly. Leg cramps have been bad all day. The change of position from wheelchair to bed helped

for a while, but now his only relief will come when the sleeping

medicine knocks him out. Tears are running down my face and I'm

praying quietly. "Lord, why do you let him keep living in pain?

Take him home, pleeease." I was finally ready to let him go.

In what may be the most common picture of our lifestyle,

Ralph is parked in front of the TV in his wheelchair watching daily

re-runs of old sit-coms. He chuckles at the antics of Deputy Barney

Fife or Mr. Ed, the talking horse. For evening entertainment, we

discovered M.A.S.H. as the series was nearing the close of its 11-

year run. Weekends Ralph usually picked sports. Golf was a

sleeper, though the scenery was nice when he woke up. Baseball

became his favorite thing to watch on TV. It was new and current,

unlike well-worn comedies where he anticipated every line.

The Phillies were doing well. I upgraded the cable so Ralph

could watch a Phillies game almost every day. I would be in the

kitchen, hear Ralph chuckle, hear the crowd noise and the

announcer's excited voice. Then I knew the Phillies had made a

run or a good defensive play. I'd get to his side in time to see the

re-play. We started staying up late to watch extra-inning games

and sometimes even West-coast games. Focusing on a game kept

the leg cramps at bay, and that was worth the loss of sleep. When the Phillies won the 2008 World Series, we both enjoyed the celebration.

Memories of our three committed attendant care workers are precious. But even the most reliable helpers have their own lives, and stuff happens. Maria eventually had to find a new full time job and was unable to coordinate it with Ralph's hours. Doris retired in her eighties. And then one Tuesday, our old companion and friend Florence didn't show up.

While doing Ralph's care myself, I attempted to call her home phone and cell phone and even her church to find her. That afternoon, acting on a desperate hunch, I tracked her down at Temple University Hospital, where they would tell me nothing except that she was in the neuro-intensive-care unit. Two days later, I was relieved to hear from Florence herself and one of her sisters. She had had a seizure on Sunday and even her family didn't know where she was. She had talked about retiring someday, but not that way.

Replacing Florence proved to be an impossible task. Young recruits sent by Attendant Care were un-committed or had unreliable transportation. Older ones wanted things their way and became annoyed at changes or my reminders about duties. Most of them never talked to Ralph and seemed to regard him as an object rather than a person. One had failed the required criminal background check. There were often un-filled days when we depended on our only emergency back-up—me.

At the same time, volunteer help with Ralph's range-of-motion exercises was dwindling. We had to rearrange the schedule and cut down the frequency after he had the feeding tube and began liquid feedings. Some of our volunteers could not continue with the new times. Often, instead of a team of two volunteers, we had one who would work with an attendant—or with me.

I felt the physical strain. Painful sciatica pervaded my caretaking duties and sent me to the doctor who prescribed physical therapy for my back. Eighteen months of that fixed the problem and taught me how to prevent further bouts. It also made me acutely aware that I could not keep taking care of Ralph indefinitely. A day might come when my illness or injury would necessitate putting him in a nursing home.

I explored retirement communities for both of us. The conclusion from that search was that since Ralph already needed skilled nursing care, our assets were not sufficient and most communities would not admit us. I began taking my Social Security to supplement his disability pay and prayed, "Lord, help me take care of him at home for as long as he needs it.

A happy scene from those years is of family crowded into the small dining room for a big dinner. Thanksgiving was our favorite family holiday. Eddie and Kay arrived Thanksgiving Day from Pittsburgh bringing pies and Ed's green tomato pickles. Jenny and her family came Wednesday and helped with the set-up. I made traditional sides ahead of time—sauerkraut salad, molded cranberry salad, heavenly rice. In the big dinner scene, Ralph is parked beside the table with a pole next to him which holds the bag of his liquid feeding. He enjoys the dinner smells, conversation and laughter, even though he can't sample the food, and he has his brother's company for the weekend to watch TV.

Friends for Ralph were bright spots in the plodding weekly routine. In my kaleidoscope of scenes, the picture of John and Ralph in the living room playing chess on Tuesday afternoons is clear. John had a custom table made for the chess board. It fit between the leg rests of the wheelchair and was the perfect height to give Ralph a clear view of the whole board. John would reach across the board and take Ralph's hand to get his responses about moves.

Later, John started coming on Thursday evenings as well to watch comedy videos with him. When he heard Ralph liked M.A.S.H., he bought the complete set of DVD's. Over several years, they watched all eleven seasons, two episodes at a time, and laughed together or, I suspect, shed a few tears together. After M.A.S.H. they began working on the 1950's Lone Ranger series. I can still picture Ralph sitting up in bed with John in a chair beside him leaning in close, remote in hand.

Other men who came to help with exercise were a welcome change for Ralph from the female caregivers who surrounded him. He enjoyed the different perspectives they brought into the conversation as they worked. Topics ranged from engineering jokes to sports, current events, and theology—exercise for the mind as well as the body. When volunteers were at an all-time low, the Lord provided two new ones with fresh outlooks and refreshing energy.

One of them, Steve T., an enthusiastic Phillies fan, decided we needed to take Ralph to a Phillies game. He did the research, bought tickets for an afternoon game, drove us in our van to the ball park, and sat in the right field handicapped section with Ralph and me, pointing out sights and commenting on what was going on all around. We left a little early when the sun moved in and it began to get too hot. Ralph indicated he definitely wanted to do it again.

The next year, we set out to do just that. We picked a game early in the season when it should be cooler. But, Philly heat and humidity arrived early that year. I had the van in the shop for two days the week before the game because the engine was running hot. They fixed the problem just in time for our trip to the ball park. Or did they?

Game day arrived with a forecast high of 95, but Ralph said he wanted to try it anyway, even if we could only stay a couple innings. On the way, the van overheated in Ardmore. Thanks to the previous week's experience, I knew exactly what to do: turn off the air conditioning, turn on the heater (!) full blast to draw heat out of the engine, find a safe shady place to pull over, turn off the engine and wait. Thank God we had taken back roads and were not stuck in traffic on the Schuylkill Expressway!

When the van had cooled a bit and Ralph was getting dangerously hot, we made our way slowly to Steve's house which was five minutes away. There, we watched the game in air-conditioned comfort on Steve's big screen TV, ate his food, and had plenty of cold drinks and ice to cool Ralph down. On TV, we saw Steve's wife and brother sweltering in their premium seats behind home plate. About the seventh inning, a horrific storm went through the city wreaking havoc at the ball park. We saw that on TV as well—panicked fans trying to flee, being hit by flying debris and trash cans. Thank God we were not there! By dark, the van was completely cooled and we made it safely home without further incident.

That was how our van decision dilemma of 2010 began. The problem was that the oil pan under the engine was rusting out. The fix would cost thousands. The parts were no longer available for a 15-year old vehicle; they would have to come off a junked van. Our mechanic said, "We can keep fixing this for you IF we can get the parts, but you need something more reliable." I appreciated his honesty. Steve T. said, "If it were a horse, I would shoot it." I needed his humor.

Proverbs 16:3-4a says, "Commit to the Lord whatever you do and your plans will succeed. The Lord works out everything for his own ends." Committing all to the Lord and trusting him to lead, I began in my "spare" time to research vans and weigh options. There were many more kinds of vans available than there had been 15 years earlier, including more fuel-efficient—and more expensive—mini-vans. We would have to deplete savings, take out a loan, and still need more money. Was it worth it? We could just limp along with the old van. However it was becoming unsafe even to take Ralph to church or me to the grocery store.

Ralph had been a quad for 32 years. He had grown more sensitive to colds and prone to infections. Each new bout with illness led anew to the realization that this one could do him in. How long could he continue?

I was wearing down, strength and energy diminishing. Losing long-time help had been disheartening. Training and supervising new help seemed to take most of my time and constant vigilance. "What if" I can't do it was a real concern. How long could I continue?

Should I deplete savings and put us in debt in order to buy a vehicle that might not be needed for as long as the loan terms? A reliable van could make Ralph's last years or months or weeks more enjoyable for him. It would be easier for me to take him out more. To be honest, _would_ I take him out more? Not if I didn't get more sleep and more help. I came to the conclusion we had two options. Plan A: take out a loan and spend more than 30,000 on a conversion mini-van. Or Plan B: try to find a make-do van of any kind for less than 20,000. Ralph preferred Plan B. His frugal nature did not like debt.

The solution was neither Plan A nor B, but Plan G! God's Plan began to unfold in August. We were approved for a low-interest loan through the Pennsylvania Assistive Technology Fund. Steve and others from church began raising money to pay down the loan. Gifts came in from other sources to help with a down-payment. The conversion dealer found a used 2008 low-mileage mini-van and sent it out for a new rear-entry adaptation. And my "Is it worth it?" question was answered by the following note, hand written on the back of a bulletin insert and handed to me as we were walking out of church on August 8, 2010.

"Ralph and Nancy:

I want you both to know what a tremendous, constant testimony the 2 of you are to me. I know your normal day presents a lot of challenges that I don't experience & don't have to deal *with. Yet here you are, Lord's Day after Lord's Day, faithfully coming to worship, and you Nancy being so supportive and consistent ministering to Ralph. If I were in your position, Ralph, I could easily imagine just saying any given Sunday, 'Why bother?' or 'It's just too much.' But you haven't given up.*

We need you, Ralph; we need you, Nancy. You encourage us to keep going, and trust more consistently in the faithfulness of God Who never gives up on us, & gives us what we need.

Thank you both!!

s. Larry A."

September 28, I signed the loan papers. October 1, we picked up the 2008 Dodge Grand Caravan with new rear-entry ramp conversion. On a bright and sunny October 13, I took Ralph to Home Depot just for the experience and pushed him up and down those immense aisles looking at everything. The DIY superstore did not exist 32 years before when he was DIY-ing. He would have been a regular customer. Between August and November, 2010, over $25,000 in gifts for the van were received through the church. The loan was paid off December 13. Thank you, Lord, for your generous blessings!

Chapter 29 Finishing the Race, Keeping the Faith

Our God is a multi-tasker. While executing his plan to bless us with the van, he was already at work on our problem of unreliable help. That involved working in other people's lives as well. In late October, I detailed the needs in a written prayer. By June 2011, the Lord had solved all the help issues: He provided a good attendant with child-care so she could work more hours; he removed a problem attendant so I didn't have to fire her (a task I hate); he provided another good one with needed car repairs so she could get here; and he supplied two new caring and committed attendants through ads in our church bulletin. "Praise you, Jesus!" I wrote. "This may be our best 'staff' ever!"

Patterns in a kaleidoscope appear most clearly when viewed against a bright light source. The pictures of God's blessings were like those bright patterns—his care and material provision, faithful helpers, friends, family times, insights from his Word. But clouds on the horizon began rolling in, darkening the shapes and dimming the scenes. In 2011, the Phillies were declining and so was Ralph. Baseball no longer provided an entertaining distraction from pain. We went to another game early in the season. Bumping along over the pavement at the ball park started a series of wheelchair repair issues. Like the old van, the chair was wearing out and the parts to fix it were no longer available.

There were medical supply issues also. Manufacturers stopped making or changed some catheter and feeding supplies that had worked for us for years. We had to experiment with and find new ones. Changes in Medicare limited the choices and changed the suppliers we were allowed to use. A supplier less than four miles away was no longer allowed to deliver, but had to ship heavy cases of food by UPS through a shipping center five miles away in the opposite direction. It made no sense.

My mental images of Ralph from those days were troubling. His head drooped more. His eyes drooped, too. He was not able to use the Eyegaze System at all. His hand squeeze grew weaker and weaker. His expression was sad, and he smiled less. A Phillies homerun didn't get much reaction from him, but then there were fewer homeruns to react to. Because of his leg spasms, two people were often needed to manage his care and turn him. Most nights, I worked with the attendant to give his enema and position him in bed.

Always in the background were my own health concerns. My hands for one. They were hurting almost constantly from all the pushing and pulling and gripping and squeezing and pinching I did in the process of Ralph's care. Add to that weeding and bush trimming and snow shoveling as well as housework. The joints at the bases of my thumbs were looking swollen and deformed. The primary care doctor sent me for x-rays and then to a hand specialist for cortisone injections. The diagnosis: arthritis. Cortisone injections would help for a few months at a time. Eventually, I would need surgery. Meanwhile, I welcomed the partial relief and time bought with the injections.

In early 2012, I had cataract surgery. Like many of my peers, I didn't know how much I was not seeing until the first eye was done. Then I couldn't wait to have the second one done.

Tiredness and fatigue were constant. In the long, late evenings especially, I echoed the cries of the Psalmist, "How long, O Lord, how long?" (Psalm 6:3). I added real tears to the words because of the pain in my hands.

An increase in my heart palpitations and a visual migraine episode prompted the cardiologist to send me for an ultrasound of the carotid arteries. They were fine, but the results showed some nodules on the thyroid. Another specialist consulted. More tests. A biopsy. Trusting the Lord in the scary unknown is easier said than done. Knowing that the girls in my Women's Bible Study small group were praying for me helped, but waiting was still hard.

One night, while doing my Bible study homework, the Spirit led me to Romans 15:13. "May the God of hope fill you with all joy and peace as you trust in him, so that you may overflow with hope by the power of the Holy Spirit." God was speaking his encouragement to me in those words. Tears of joy flowed as they had the very first time he spoke through his word from Isaiah 42. I emailed the group to pray that verse for me and got immediate replies from two of them that they were doing so. At the end of the days of waiting, the biopsy results were negative. Thank you, Lord, for giving me your joy and peace in the meantime.

In May of 2012, the "other" Nancy called. Nancy and Hank had taken their son Fred home in 1979 shortly after Ralph went to MossRehab. Nancy's Christmas notes were always encouraging as she wrote, "God is good," and told about Fred giving them smiles like an infant. This time she called to give me the news that Fred had gone home to the Lord on April 29. It had been 33 years that she and Hank had cared for him with the help of faithful friends from their church. We praised God together for sustaining them. I praised God for continuing to sustain me and giving me Nancy as an example and role model. When others would tell her she was a strong woman, she always replied, "No, I'm not, but I have a strong God."

Through days of declining health for Ralph and me, little rays of sunshine came from an unexpected source—93-year-old Elsie. She had seen us at church and started sending notes of encouragement. She had already sent two or three before I even met her. Each note contained a little scripture, an inspirational story, a joke, or an original poem. Her love for God flowed from each page. Every note was led by the Holy Spirit. Whatever problem we were facing, Elsie's encouragement was right on target. Finding a card from her in our mailbox always brightened the day. I read them to Ralph, saved them and re-read them often. Elsie was nearly blind and deaf.

In the fall of 2013, I had an unspoken sense that time was drawing short. We were studying 2 Corinthians in Women's Bible Study and I was preparing to teach from chapter 5 where Paul talks about longing for his heavenly dwelling. I read the passage and the talk I was writing to Ralph. His eyes were open. He seemed attentive, though he could not raise his head or eyes to look at me. I took his hand and asked him if he, too, was looking forward to his heavenly dwelling? He squeezed my hand. That was the last definite response he ever gave to anything.

At Thanksgiving, Jenny also sensed that the end might be near. She spent a long time talking to him and saying goodbye before they left to go back to Alabama.

On a Monday night near the end of January, I worked with our attendant cleaning Ralph up after the enema routine. We had him lying on his side which often makes him tense because it is not a comfortable position. His legs began to tremble a bit—not an unusual response. But the trembling spread. *"What's happening?"* the attendant asked. *"He might be having a seizure."* I replied. We hurried to finish the clean-up, get a clean pad under him, and raise the head of the bed. The trembling didn't stop. It got worse. I grabbed the phone and punched in 911.

The kaleidoscope began spinning in a rapid blur. *EMT's struggling to start an IV to give medicine to stop the seizure.* Our evening attendant left; the night one named Karen arrived. She went with us to the hospital, and I was glad to have her company. *Following the ambulance.* It's funny how we got all the green lights. (Do ambulance drivers have the power to do that?) *All night in the ER.* They couldn't find an appropriate room for Ralph until the middle of the next day. *The seizure that wouldn't quit.* Even with heavy doses of medication, mild twitching continued. *My calm composure.* After all, I was an old hand at this emergency room thing. Only my very, very dry mouth gave away my inner turmoil. As I've said, trusting the Lord in the scary unknown is easier said than done, no matter how much practice you get.

Two scenes during more than a week in the hospital stand out. In one, Amy was visiting. She told us she had some news. She reached into her bag and pulled out a photo ID badge that said Temple University Faculty! She told us all about her new job—her dream job—and the miraculous way it had come about. It was a job with a future that could enable her to support herself and get out of debt. I praised the Lord with her.

After Amy left, I gave Ralph a hug and kissed him. "Our baby is going to make it," I said. "God has fulfilled my very first prayer after you had the brain hemorrhage; 'God, please let him live so we can watch our little girls grow up together.'" It seemed like Ralph relaxed a bit. I know I did.

The second stand-out scene took place when a technician came in with a portable machine to give Ralph an electro-encephalogram (EEG). She stuck electrodes all over his head to detect brain wave activity which could then be seen on a computer monitor. I watched with curiosity as she went through the preparations and began the test. She was very willing to answer my questions, except for the ones about what it all meant—the neurologist would have to answer those. She showed me the difference between the background resting waves and spikey apparent seizure activity.

We both noticed that when I spoke, the spikey waves appeared all over, but especially on the left side of Ralph's brain where the original injury had been. He didn't react to the technician's voice. A nurse came in to check the IV. He didn't react to her voice. Only to my voice. It seemed as though he was trying to respond to me, and the effort caused an increase in seizure activity. The technician made note of it for the doctor.

Back home again, our routine required even more vigilance. A Friend had given us some money to supplement the pay of an attendant to stay overnight and give me a little more sleep. Karen was able to fill that role, often staying all night instead of just putting him to bed as she had before the seizure. The wheelchair problem was getting worse. The tilt mechanism was slipping badly because of a worn gear bar. A friend with mechanical intuition looked at it and decided he could make something that would steady the joint and keep it from slipping. A few days later he came back to install his invention. It did the trick. And on the calendar, life went on as normal. For about a month.

Saturday, March 1st, Ralph threw up his lunch and aspirated the vomit. With the help of a neighbor, I drove him to the hospital. He was in obvious respiratory distress and hypothermic. The subsequent blur of events was dizzying. By Monday a nurse care coordinator was talking with me about hospices. Tuesday morning, Amy went with me to see an in-patient hospice in the city on top of a hill. She picked out his room with a commanding view of the city. We went back to the hospital where I signed the paperwork, and arrangements were made to transport him to the hospice that afternoon. It felt right. Ralph would be going to his heavenly home soon.

The spinning scenes stopped. A slow parade of loving faces began as old friends visited us at the hospice. They shared memories, Scripture, comfort, songs, and even funny stories. Sometimes, I was the one comforting them. If Ralph had any awareness, I'm sure he appreciated being surrounded by so many. Jenny arrived Thursday. Friday we had family time. The parade of friends had slowed by then as people sensed the end was near and allowed us privacy.

I had my own time with my husband while Jenny drove Amy to and from her apartment. I read him some of our favorite Scriptures. I talked about heaven and what it would be like. I talked about our life together and how thankful I was; how if it hadn't been for him I wouldn't have found Jesus. I told him, "I love you," many, many times. I told him it was okay for him to go to his heavenly home. Sometimes I just sat holding his hand in silence.

A nurse (two or three, in fact) encouraged us to go home each night and get some sleep. She said she had seen many patients hang on as long as a family member was there; they didn't want to die in front of loved ones. When the family finally left for a while, then they felt free to leave. We took her advice and went home each night. Saturday night, we stayed longer than usual. It just seemed that the end was very near. We settled in uncomfortably for the night. But finally, I said, "I think we need to take you kids home and put you to bed." The nurse promised to call me if there was a change. Sleep in a real bed was sorely needed at that point.

The call came about 4:00 am. Sunday, March 9, 2014.

Saturday, March 22, we had a joyous celebration of Ralph's life with lots of praise music and lots of Ralph's favorite dessert—pie—all kinds of pies made by many friends from church. The theme of the service was 2 Timothy 4:7-8.

"I have fought the good fight, I have finished the race, I have kept the faith. Now there is in store for me the crown of righteousness, which the Lord, the righteous Judge, will award to me on that day—and not only to me, but also to all who have longed for his appearing."

About People in this Book

The people whose lives have touched ours are real. In most cases, I have used their real names with their knowledge and permission. A few names were changed, because I have lost contact with them. Others were left out of the story only because there are too many to mention. We praise God for all those who have helped show us God's love and caring over the years. We pray that the Lord will bless them as they blessed us and that we will meet them again in heaven. Some have already gone there to prepare the way.

Made in the USA
Middletown, DE
12 June 2021

42018459R00146